CHILDCRAFT
THE HOW AND WHY LIBRARY

OUR EARTH

World Book, Inc.
a Scott Fetzer company
Chicago

Childcraft—The How and Why Library
(Reg. U.S. Pat. and T.M. Off.—Marca Registrada)
© 2000 World Book, Inc. All rights reserved. This volume may not
be reproduced in whole or in part in any form without prior written
permission from the publisher.

World Book, Inc.
233 N. Michigan Avenue
Chicago, IL 60601

© 1996, 1995, 1994, 1993, 1991, 1990, 1989, 1987, 1986, 1985
World Book, Inc. © 1982, 1981, 1980, 1979, World Book-Childcraft
International, Inc. © 1976, 1974, 1973, 1971, 1970, 1969, 1968, 1965,
1964 Field Enterprises Educational Corporation.

International Copyright © 1996, 1995, 1994, 1993, 1991, 1990, 1989,
1987, 1986, 1985 World Book, Inc. International Copyright © 1982,
1981, 1980, 1979 World Book-Childcraft International, Inc. International
Copyright © 1976, 1974, 1973, 1971, 1970, 1969, 1968, 1965, 1964
Field Enterprises Educational Corporation.

Childcraft—The How and Why Library ISBN 0-7166-0197-4
Our Earth ISBN 0-7166-0155-9
Library of Congress Catalog Card Number 98-75114
Printed in the United States of America
  2 3 4 5 6 7 8 9 06 05 04 03 02 01

For information on other World Book products,
visit our Web site at www.worldbook.com
For information on sales to schools and libraries in the
United States, call 1-800-975-3250.
For information on sales to schools and libraries in
Canada, call 1-800-837-5365.

Contents

Introduction

When someone asks you where you live, you probably answer with your street address or the name of your town, state, or country. But you also live in a larger place—a world called the earth, which all people share.

This book, *Our Earth,* helps you learn about the planet where we all live. You will find out what the earth is made of and why it is shaped like a ball. Then you can take a closer look at the earth. You will learn about the land, which is made up of mountains, valleys, and plains. You will learn about water that fills the earth's oceans, lakes, and rivers. And you will explore the sky.

The weather has a big effect on the earth. This book explains rain, lightning, thunder, snow, and hail. Everyone is interested in the weather sometimes, but watching the weather is actually a job for some people. You will find out more about their work in this book, and you will learn how people have tried to predict the weather in different ways over the years.

People depend on the earth's land, water, and air to live. We must use the land wisely and keep the water and air clean so that plants and animals will grow. If the world is healthy for plants and animals, it is probably a healthy place for us, too. This book tells you what people are doing to protect the earth and how you can help!

There are many features in this book to help you find your way through it. You will find fun-filled facts in the boxes marked **Know It All!** You can amaze your friends with what you learn!

This book also has many activities that you can do at home. Look for the words **Try This!** over a colored ball. The activity that follows offers a way to learn more about the earth. For example, you can grow your own rock crystals, do an experiment to see whether certain plants grow better in fresh water or salt water, or even make clouds.

Each activity has a number in its colored ball. Activities with a 1 in a green ball are simplest to do. Those with a 2 in a yellow ball may require a little adult help with cutting, measuring, or using hot water. Activities with a 3 in a red ball may need more adult help.

Know It All! boxes have fun-filled facts.

Each activity has a number. The higher the number, the more adult help you may need.

An activity that has this colorful border is a little more complex than one without the border.

5

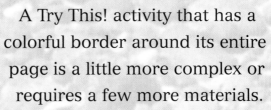

A Try This! activity that has a colorful border around its entire page is a little more complex or requires a few more materials. Read the list of materials and the instructions before you begin.

As you read this book, you will see that some words are printed in bold type, **like this.** These are words that might be new to you. Their meanings and pronunciations are in the **Glossary** at the back of the book. Turn to the **Index** to look up page numbers of subjects that interest you the most.

If you enjoy learning about the earth, find out more about it in other resources. Here are just a few. Check them out at a bookstore or at your local or school library.

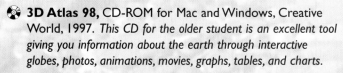

- **3D Atlas 98,** CD-ROM for Mac and Windows, Creative World, 1997. *This CD for the older student is an excellent tool giving you information about the earth through interactive globes, photos, animations, movies, graphs, tables, and charts.*

- **Dear Katie, The Volcano Is a Girl,** by Jean Craighead George, 1998. *Katie's grandmother thinks the volcano is a work of nature, but Katie believes it is that of Pele, a Hawaiian goddess.*

- **Deserts**, by Seymour Simon, 1990. *Learn about animal adaptation, "rain showers," and the movement of sand dunes in this book that is full of beautiful photographs.*

- **The Drop in My Drink,** by Meredith Hooper and Chris Coady, 1998. *Learn about the earth's water and how important it is to life.*

- **How Mountains Are Made,** by Kathleen Weidner, 1995. *This "Let's-Read-and-Find-Out Science" book uses very simple language to explain the formation of mountains.*

- **Incredible Earth,** by Nick Clifford, 1996. *This well-illustrated volume tells you about fossils, wind, oceans, coral reefs, deserts, buried treasures, and much, much more.*

- **Lightning**, by Peter Murray, 1995. *Did you know that lightning is important to our planet?*

- **Making the World,** by Douglas Wood, 1998. *Take a trip around the world to see how everything in nature works together.*

- **One Less Fish,** by Kim Michelle Toft and Allan Sheater, 1998. *An easy-to-read book that explores what's happening to the fish.*

- **Squishy, Misty, Damp & Muddy,** by Mollie Cone, 1996. *Learn how important wetlands are to people.*

- **Storm Chaser: Into the Eye of a Hurricane,** by Keith Elliot Greenberg, 1998. *Brian, a pilot for the National Oceanic and Atmospheric Administration, teaches you a lot about hurricanes as he tells you about his job.*

- **You're Aboard Spaceship Earth,** by Patricia Lauber, 1996. *The spaceship you are on is Earth, and it has everything on it that you need to survive.*

Planet Earth

Look up in the sky. You see the stars, the moon, and a whole lot of "nothing." But that "nothing" is really something called space. Did you know that you are riding along in space on a large, blue ball called the planet earth?

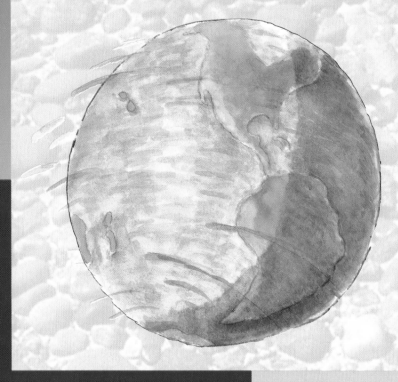

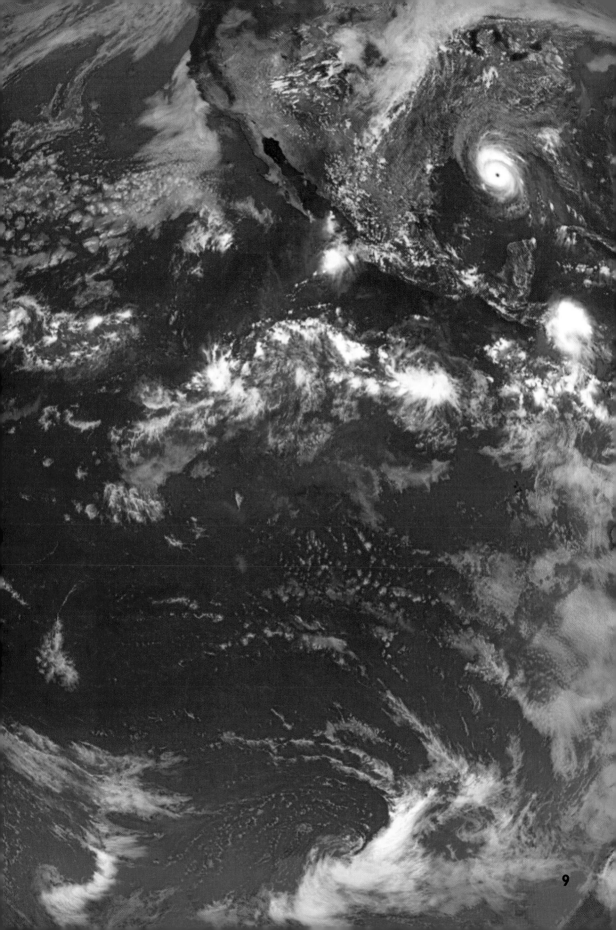

The Spinning World

Did you ever think you could spin around and around without getting dizzy? Well, that's what happens to you every day and every night. The earth is spinning around like a huge top, and you're along for the ride!

Both the earth and a top spin around an axis, like a wheel spins around its axle. See for yourself. Push a stick through a ball of clay. Twirl the stick, and the ball will spin around.

Now imagine a pole going through the center of the earth. That imaginary pole is called the earth's axis. One end of the

The earth spins around like this top. The time it takes the earth to make one complete turn is about 24 hours—one full day and night.

earth's axis is called the North Pole. The other end is called the South Pole. The earth spins around its axis, like a wheel spins around its axle.

People can't feel the earth turn because it is so big. But we know it does turn because that's what gives us our day and night. In the morning, when the sky is bright, we know that our part of the earth is turned toward the sun. At night, when the sky is dark, we know that we've turned away from the sun.

TRY THIS!

Make a round clay ball to be the earth. Mark a small X on the ball to show the place where you live on the earth. Stick a pencil through the ball. In a dark room, shine a flashlight on your earth. The flashlight will be the sun. Turn the earth slowly and watch what happens where you live. When is it daytime? When is it night? What if the earth didn't spin?

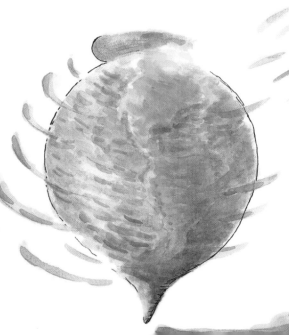

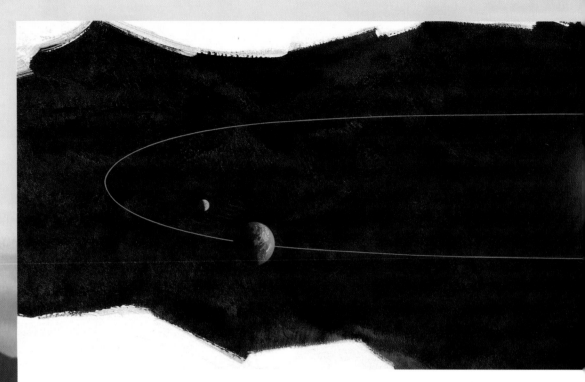

Moving Around the Sun

The earth travels around the sun in a large almost perfect circle.

The earth does more than just spin. As it spins, it moves through space.

The earth travels around the sun at a speed of about 66,600 miles (107,200 kilometers) an hour. But it isn't moving in a straight line. Instead, it whirls around the sun in a large, almost perfect circle. This path the earth takes around the sun

TRY THIS!

2 Ask a grown-up to help you try this activity outside, a safe distance from people. Put a small rubber ball into the toe of an old, long sock. Hold the other end of the sock and whirl the ball around your head. Feel how the ball is trying to pull away? But you and the sock have a bigger pull, like the sun's pull that keeps the earth in its orbit. While you are still whirling the sock, let go of it. What happens? The ball flies away. This is what would happen to the earth if the pull of the sun's gravity suddenly stopped.

is called an orbit (AWR biht).

What keeps the earth moving around the sun? Why doesn't it move all over space?

Everything in space pulls at everything else. This pull is called **gravity** (GRAV uh tee). The bigger a thing is, the stronger its pull. The sun is more than a million times bigger than the earth, so it tugs hard at the earth. It is this strong tug that keeps the earth in orbit.

The time it takes the earth to go all the way around the sun is a little more than 365 days. This is what we call a year.

Why Is the Earth Shaped Like a Ball?

Why is the earth shaped like a ball? Why isn't it round and flat like a pancake or square like a block? Why does it spin? And why does it whirl around the sun?

Most scientists think the answers lie in the earth's beginning. They think it began billions of years ago with a gigantic, spinning cloud of dust and gas in space.

Most scientists think that long ago there was a cloud, millions of miles wide. Gravity pulled it into the shape of a giant flat wheel, and it spun around and around.

As it spun, gravity slowly pulled the cloud of dust and gas together. Most of the gas collected in the middle of the cloud. It formed a lump that got bigger and bigger. As it grew bigger, its gravity became stronger. Because its pull of gravity was the same in all directions, the lump squeezed into a round ball. This gigantic ball of gas in the middle of the cloud was the beginning of the sun.

Farther out in the gigantic cloud, other balls formed as gravity pulled bits of dust and gas together. After a while, most of the cloud was used up. There were only balls of gas and dust, whirling around the sun. Scientists say these balls were the beginning of the earth and the other planets and their moons.

There are lots of clouds of dust and gas in space right now. Scientists say some of them are turning into new stars. Since our sun is a star, many scientists think that our sun and its planets began the same way.

The earth was one of the balls that formed from the dust and gas. As the earth's gravity pulled in more and more dust and gas, everything squeezed together, tighter and tighter. The ball grew hotter and hotter. It became so hot that bits of dust, mostly rock and metals, melted together. The earth glowed!

The outside of the earth didn't stay hot. The melted rock cooled. As it cooled, it

At one time, the earth was so hot it glowed.

hardened. It became a ball of hard rock and metal, as it is today. But the inside of the earth never cooled. The center of the earth is fiery hot. Heat is always flowing from it, and parts of it are still melting.

Bit by bit, we are finding new clues about the earth's beginning. There are lots of stories and beliefs of how the earth began. But nobody really knows exactly what happened.

Today the outside of the earth is cool.
But the inside is still fiery hot.

The Outside of the Earth

Take a walk and touch the outside of the earth with your feet. Dig a small hole and feel the soil. Splash in a stream. Take a deep breath of the air that surrounds you.

You live on the surface of the earth. The surface, or crust, of the earth is made of rock. In some places, it is covered with soil. In many places, it is covered with water. All around it is air.

Most people live on huge pieces of land called continents. A continent is a huge platform of rock that sticks up higher than the rest of the earth's rocky crust.

Some people live on smaller pieces of land called islands. Some islands are the tops of underwater mountains or volcanoes. Other islands are formed of sand or coral. Still others are pieces of land that have become separated from a continent.

The continents and islands are surrounded by water. Water covers almost three-fourths of the earth's surface.

You can see and touch the outside of the earth. You can feel the soil, see the water, and breathe the air that surrounds the earth.

What's Inside the Earth?

Could you dig a hole to the other side of the earth? No, it's not possible. The center of the earth is about 4,000 miles (6,400 kilometers) beneath your feet. So it's almost 8,000 miles (13,000 kilometers) to the other side of the earth. It's too far to dig. And for most of that distance, the earth is either solid rock or metal so hot that it's melted! Nobody could dig through that!

But if people could dig a hole through the earth, they would first have to go through a shell of rock. This rock formed long ago, when the outside of the earth

Digging into the earth is easy at first, but no one could dig all the way to the other side.

The earth is made up of four layers of rock. Each layer is hotter than the last.

inner core
outer core
mantle
crust

cooled down. This rock is called the earth's crust. The oceans and the continents cover the crust.

Under the crust is another layer of rock. It is called the mantle. The mantle is made of a different kind of rock than the crust. The deeper the mantle goes, the hotter it gets. At its bottom, it is hot enough to melt iron.

Beneath the mantle is a layer of melted metal—metal so hot that it's thick like syrup! This layer is called the outer core.

In the very center of the earth is the inner core. It's a ball of hot, solid, squeezed-together metal.

The earth makes different kinds of rock.

The Rock Factory

This sparkly rock is called granite. It is an igneous rock.

The earth is a huge rock factory. Scientists believe it has been making rocks for billions of years.

The earth makes three kinds of rocks. One kind is made from hot, syrupy liquid rock, deep inside the earth. The melted rock is called molten (MOHL tuhn) rock. Sometimes, some of this

liquid rock pushes its way between two layers of solid rock, making a sort of rock sandwich. Then the liquid cools and becomes solid, too. Other times, when volcanoes erupt, some of the liquid rock is pushed up out of the earth. When it reaches the earth's surface, it cools and becomes solid.

This type of rock that was once a hot liquid is called igneous (IHG nee uhs) rock. *Igneous* means "formed by fire." Granite, the gray rock used on the outside of many buildings, is an igneous rock. And so is the black, glassy rock called obsidian that some prehistoric people made into arrowheads.

Another kind of rock is made out of "rock powder." Wind and rain wear away bits of larger rocks. Rivers carry the powdery bits to the ocean. There,

TRY THIS!

1 When you visit the seaside or countryside, look for different kinds of rocks. See how many you can find. Wash each rock. See how it looks when it's wet and when it's dry. Study each rock. Does it have layers? Does it have shiny crystals? Is it rough or smooth? Store your rocks in an egg carton. How many different ways can you sort your collection?

with other bits of things, they sink to the ocean floor and form a layer called **sediment** (SEHD uh muhnt). *Sediment* comes from a word that means "to settle." Over thousands of years, the bottom layers of powder are squeezed together by the weight of new layers. Slowly, the powdery bits on the bottom are turned into a layer of solid rock. Over millions of years, earthquakes and other forces may lift up the layers of new rock until they become dry land.

Rocks that are made this way are called sedimentary rocks. Limestone and sandstone are sedimentary rocks.

The third kind of rock is made deep inside the earth. The heat and the weight of other rocks slowly change these rocks into a different kind of rock. Their new form is called metamorphic (MEHT uh MAWR fihk) rock. Metamorphic means "changed."

This rock is known as sandstone. It is a sedimentary rock.

This rock is called marble. It is a metamorphic rock that changed from limestone.

Marble is a metamorphic rock that changed from limestone. Slate is a metamorphic rock that was changed from mud. Most metamorphic rocks are very old. They stay underground unless **erosion** (ih ROH zuhn), an earthquake, or a new mountain brings them to the earth's surface.

All the rocks you see were made long, long ago. The oldest rocks ever found on the earth are more than 3 billion years old. But the earth hasn't stopped making rocks. It's making them right now. It's always wearing away old rocks and building up new ones.

Minerals Everywhere

It takes a lot of ingredients to make cookies—flour, milk, eggs, butter, sugar. Everything is all mixed together. A rock is like that. Rocks are mixtures of materials called minerals. There are about 2,000 kinds of minerals. Some are hard, some are soft, some are shiny, some are sparkly. Many of them are mixed with other minerals. But some are found in chunks, small lumps, or broad patches between layers of other kinds of rocks.

Most kinds of minerals are made up of tiny shapes called crystals. Crystals have flat sides and sharp corners. The salt we put on food is a mineral called

Graphite (GRAF yt) is a soft and slippery mineral with flat layers that slide over one another. Pencil lead is made with graphite so it can slide easily over paper while leaving a mark behind.

salt

26

Mercury comes from a red ore called cinnabar that is found near volcanoes and hot springs.

quartz

halite. It is made up of crystals shaped like cubes. Quartz crystals have beautiful pointed shapes. Sulfur crystals look like chunks of bright yellow glass. Pure mercury is a mineral that stays melted, even when cool. Mercury is used in some thermometers. Uranium has flat sides and a dull color. It is never found alone, but always is mixed with other minerals. Uranium is sometimes used as a fuel in making electricity.

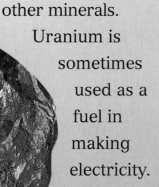

sulfur

uranium

What Is the Giant's Causeway?

Ancient stories say that a king built the Giant's Causeway and that he had to use stones large enough for giants to walk on them.

On the coast of Northern Ireland, 40,000 mysterious columns of stone rise out of the sea like huge stairs. The unusual rocks cover a length of beach about 3 miles (5 kilometers) long! They are called the Giant's Causeway.

Ancient stories tell about a king who built a causeway of stepping stones between two countries. The stones joined Ireland and Scotland and had to be large enough for giants to walk on them.

It is not surprising that people long ago invented such a story, because the real stones on Northern Ireland's coast are very strange. Each measures about 18 inches (46 centimeters) across the top. And every one of them has six sides. They look as if they must have been made by human beings, but they were not. They were made by a volcano.

The Giant's Causeway was actually formed by a volcano.

Long ago, **magma** exploded from deep inside the earth. As it cooled, it shrank into a hard rock called basalt. As it became cold, the rock split into long columns.

In Northern Ireland, the columns have six sides, but basalt columns found elsewhere may have only four or five sides. A whole cliff of basalt columns can be found in central California. It is called the Devil's Postpile and looks like a giant's supply of fence posts.

TRY THIS!
2

Grow Your Own Crystals

It seems strange to think of hard, lifeless things growing, but crystals actually do grow. They grow by joining together. For example, the walls of a cave may be covered with a particular mineral. Water trickling down the walls washes crystals of this mineral onto the cave floor. The water, filled with many tiny crystals, forms a puddle on the floor. As the puddle slowly dries up, the crystals stick together. They form larger crystals. Here's how you can grow your own crystals.

You Will Need:

a pipe cleaner
a glass
1/2 cup (120 ml)
   hot tap water
salt
a spoon
a pencil
a magnifying glass

What To Do:

1. Bend one end of the pipe cleaner into an interesting shape. Twist the other end onto the middle of a pencil.

2. Have an adult pour the hot tap water into the glass.

3. Put several spoonfuls of salt into the water. Stir after each spoonful. Stop when you see that the salt is not dissolving any more.

4. Lay the pencil across the top of the glass. Make sure that your pipe cleaner shape is dangling in the hot water.

5. Carefully set the glass in a place where you know it will not be disturbed for several days.

6. After a few hours, look through the glass at the pipe cleaner. You should see crystals growing on it.

7. After a few days, when the water is mostly gone, carefully slip the pipe cleaner off the pencil. Don't touch the crystals— they are very delicate.

8. Now you can look at the crystals with a magnifying glass. Try to see the flat surfaces and angles. If you like, you can hang up your crystal creation as a decoration. Write down what happened to your crystals.

natural and
polished
opal

Precious Stones

natural and
polished
diamond

They shine, they sparkle, they flash and shimmer. They are only stones, small pieces of minerals, but they are so beautiful and hard to find that they are precious (PREHSH uhs). Precious means "having great value." Diamonds, rubies, emeralds, sapphires, and opals are examples of precious stones or gems.

Diamonds come from deep inside the earth. They are buried in rock that is in or near volcanoes that are no longer erupting. When first taken from the ground, diamonds are dull and grayish. After they are cut and polished, they sparkle.

polished
and natural
sapphire

A diamond is the hardest of all things. It is so hard that it can even cut rocks. The only thing that can scratch a diamond is another diamond.

32

polished and natural ruby

Corundum is a common mineral. But when tiny bits of other minerals are added, it becomes a precious stone. With a bit of titanium and iron mixed in, it becomes a clear, blue sapphire. With chromium mixed in, it becomes a dark red ruby. With beryl mixed in, it becomes a deep green emerald.

natural and polished emerald

Birthstones
This table shows the gem or gems accepted by most jewelers as the birthstone for each month.

January	February
garnet	amethyst
March	**April**
aquamarine	diamond
bloodstone	
May	**June**
emerald	pearl moonstone
	alexandrite
July	**August**
ruby	peridot sardonyx
September	**October**
sapphire	opal
	tourmaline
November	**December**
topaz	zircon turquoise

What Is Ore?

iron

Metals are found in earth's rocks. In order to use the metal, the kind of rock that contains the metal must be mined, or dug out of the ground. This rock that contains the metal is called ore.

Many ores are found beneath the ground in layers of rock called veins. Iron ore is mined. After it is mined,

silver

This is a vein of quartz between layers of granite.

34

the ore is smelted. Smelting removes metal from the ore. The ore is put into a huge furnace and mixed with other rocks. Hot air is blasted into the furnace. When the furnace is hot enough, the liquid iron sinks to the bottom. It then is poured into a car that holds many tons of molten, or melted, iron.

bauxite

Steel is made by heating iron and mixing it with a small amount of a chemical called carbon. Steel is used to make such things as automobile parts, buildings, screws, and paper clips.

Aluminum is light, strong, and doesn't rust. It comes from an ore called bauxite (BAWK syt). To make aluminum, the compound called alumina must be removed from the bauxite. Aluminum is used for many things, including pots and pans, airplane parts, and chewing gum wrappers.

gold

Gold and silver ores are hard to find and sometimes are found as natural metals. Both are heavy, but very soft. Gold and silver are used in coins and jewelry.

What Are Fossils?

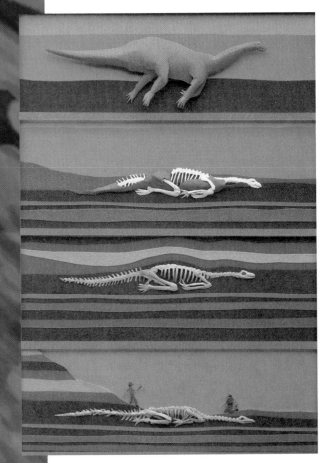

It took years and years for dinosaur bones to become the fossils that scientists uncover today.

Imagine a giant dinosaur moving along a lakeshore 80 million years ago. It is searching for food. The dinosaur sees some plants and wades out to them. But before it reaches the plants, it steps into a deep hole filled with soft, wet mud. The dinosaur sinks deeper and deeper into the mud, and the dinosaur drowns.

Over time, the soft parts of the animal's body rot away. Only its bones are left, covered by mud. For many years, layers of sediment pile on top of the mud and pack it tightly around the bones. Eventually, the packed mud turns to clay. After many more years pass, the clay turns to rock.

During all this time, minerals in the water of the lake fill the hollow places in the bones. The minerals harden and the skeleton of the dinosaur is preserved. The bones in the rock are called **fossils** (FAHS uhlz).

Other animals or plants can become fossils too when they are buried in sediment. After the sediment turns to rock, only the print of the animal remains.

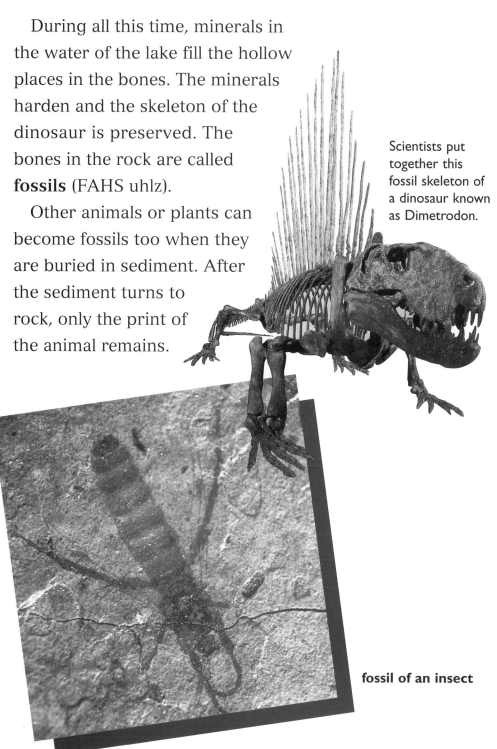

Scientists put together this fossil skeleton of a dinosaur known as Dimetrodon.

fossil of an insect

Make Fossil Prints

It takes the earth a long, long time to make the print of a fossil. But you can make prints like fossil prints much more quickly.

You Will Need:

a chunk of modeling clay
a pie pan
a leaf, twig, or sea shell
a large paper cup
1 cup (240 ml) of plaster
  of Paris
1/2 cup (120 ml) of water
a stick for stirring

What To Do:

1. Put the clay on the pie pan. Flatten it until it is about 1 inch (2.5 centimeters) thick.

2. Press the leaf, twig, or sea shell into the clay. Remove it. If the print isn't clear, begin again.

3. Mix the plaster of Paris and water in the large paper cup with the stick. Pour the mixture into the pie pan on top of the clay.

4. Let the plaster dry about 2-3 hours. Pop the clay and plaster out of the pan. Carefully peel the clay off to find your instant "fossil."

Now that you know how to make fossil prints, ask an adult to help you search for some real ones. Some places to search are empty lots, riverbanks, the seashore, mountainsides, streambeds, or a petrified forest.

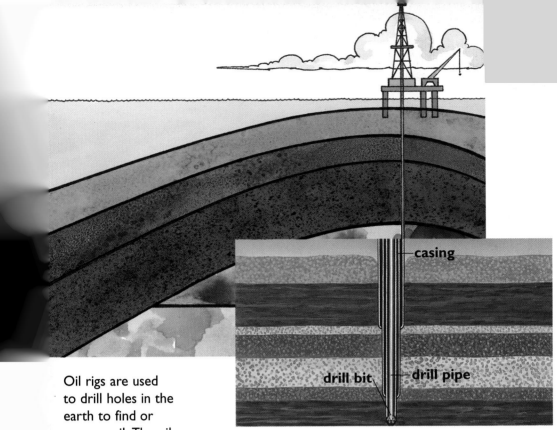

casing

drill bit   drill pipe

Oil rigs are used to drill holes in the earth to find or remove oil. The oil rig stands on legs fixed firmly on the seabed, and the drill reaches down through the middle.

What Is Oil?

Maybe you have used oil on your bicycle chain to keep it from squeaking. Did you know that oil was once part of the earth? It starts as a thick dark liquid called crude oil that is found between layers of rock deep inside the earth's crust. Crude oil is also called petroleum.

Crude oil is a fossil fuel. This means that it started forming millions of years ago from dead plants and animals that had lived in the ocean. Over millions of years, these dead plants and animals piled up on the ocean floor. Thick layers of sand and soil covered them. The sand and soil squeezed together under their own weight and the weight of the water pressing down on them. They were pressed so hard that they turned into rock. Scientists believe that the weight of the rock helped turn the piles of dead stuff into oil.

People today use oil for many things. They use oil to heat homes and to run automobiles, planes, trains, ships, and trucks. They also use oil to make such things as medicines and plastics.

The top of this oil rig has all the machinery needed to drive its drill deep into the ocean floor.

Oil companies get oil by drilling into the earth's crust. They pump out the oil that is trapped under the earth's surface. They even pump oil from under the ocean floor.

Because of its many uses, oil has become very valuable. But it takes millions of years for the earth to make more oil, so we need to make sure we don't waste it.

Who Studies the Earth?

Some of the world's best detectives are the people who study the earth. They are called geologists (jee AHL uh jihsts).

Geologists help us learn about the earth's **resources** and how to care for them. They tell us to preserve these resources and how to use them properly when we must. Some geologists study where to build homes, bridges, and dams safely. These scientists also work to protect people from earthquakes, floods, and other natural disasters.

geologist collecting lava sample

Geologists may be found chipping rocks on a mountainside or drilling on the ocean floor. Sometimes geologists work indoors. They X-ray rock samples, do research and tests on computers, or make maps of places they want to explore.

Geologists may travel all over the world. They search mountains, swamps, deserts, and the bottom of the ocean so we can learn more about the earth. They may tramp through rain forests, go underground into mines, or climb around an icy glacier.

Geologists and many other kinds of scientists uncover the secrets of the earth in different ways. Sometimes they are called earth scientists.

environmental geologist testing soil

Environmental geologists

work to solve problems of **pollution.** They search for the best ways to get rid of hazardous waste—materials that are dangerous to our health.

KNOW It All!

The word geology comes from two Greek words. *Ge* means "earth" and *logos* means "study."

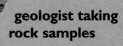

geologist taking rock samples

43

Meteorologists (MEE tee awr AHL uh jihsts) study the weather and the air that surrounds the earth.

Mining geologists study the earth's rocks and ways to remove them.

Mineralogists (mihn ur AHL uh jihsts) identify the many minerals found on the earth.

Petroleum geologists search for oil and natural gas on land and beneath the ocean floor.

Seismologists (syz MAHL uh jihsts) study the motion of the earth. They watch for earthquakes. Most earthquakes occur underwater.

geochemist experimenting with grains

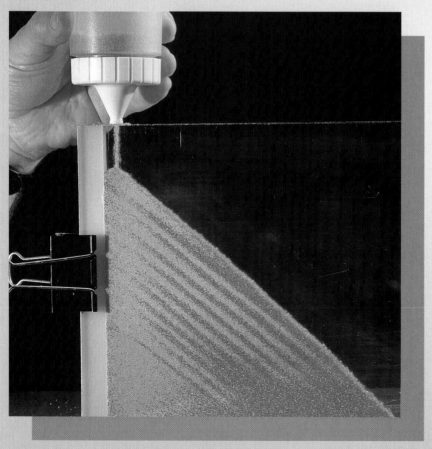

44

petroleum geologists looking for oil

Geochemists (jee oh KEHM ihsts) study the chemicals in the earth's crust, its waters, and its **atmosphere.**

Paleontologists (PAY lee uhn TAHL uh jihsts) study fossils to learn about the earth's past.

There are many kinds of earth scientists, but they have one thing in common. They all enjoy studying the earth and want to uncover its secrets.

paleontologists
uncovering fossils

Land on the Earth

The earth is a huge ball, but it is not smooth all over like a ball that you bounce or roll. The earth's surface is full of bumps and dips, but some parts of it are smooth. Where there's no water, there is land.

Some of the earth's surface is on the ocean floor. You live on one of the earth's continents—or maybe on an island. You may live on a mountain, in a valley, on a plain, or in a desert.

The Earth's Plates

It may seem that the earth's crust is one gigantic piece of rock. But the outer shell of the earth is divided into about 30 large and small pieces that fit together like a puzzle. These pieces are called tectonic (tehk TAHN ihk) plates.

The plates move on a very hot layer of rock within the mantle. The plates move very slowly, only from 1/2 to 8 inches (1.3 to 20 centimeters) per year.

Heat from inside the earth causes the mantle to rise. As this melted rock breaks through the crust, it cools and hardens, pushing the plates on either side away from each other.

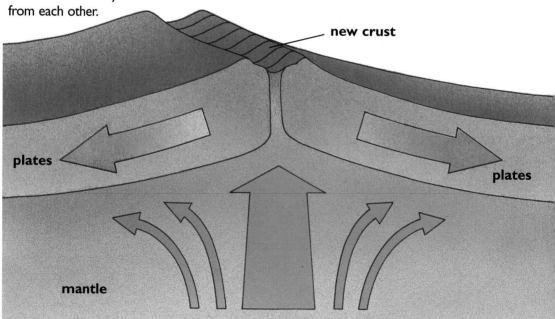

new crust

plates

plates

mantle

The continents sit on top of the plates. When the plates move, they take the continents with them. But the plates aren't only under the continents. They are also under the ocean floor. They are under water on the continents, such as lakes and rivers, too.

Under land, the plates are about 60 miles (100 kilometers) thick in most places. In some places in the ocean, they may be less than 5 miles (8 kilometers) thick.

As the plates move, the continents and oceans slowly change. Scientists think that in 50 million years, South America and Africa will be farther apart. They think the Atlantic Ocean will be wider, and the Pacific Ocean will be smaller.

200 million years ago

135 million years ago

today

Scientists believe that 200 million years ago, all the continents were joined together. Over the years, as the tectonic plates have moved, they've taken the continents with them. They are still moving today.

Why Are There Mountains?

Some mountains are no more than steep hills covered with grass and trees. Others rise high into the **atmosphere** with snow-covered peaks. Often mountains stretch out in long chains called mountain ranges.

The Cascade Mountain Range stretches across Washington.

Mountains are formed over long periods by tremendous forces in the earth. These forces move parts of the earth's crust in different ways, making different kinds of mountains.

Mountain ranges are important because they influence the **climate** and waterflow of the land around them. How do they do this? Air cools as it reaches high **altitudes** (AL tuh toodz). And cold air holds less water than warm air does. So as the warm air turns cooler near the tops of the mountains, it releases water in the form of rain or snow. This rain or snow feeds nearby rivers and streams. Mountains are also important as homes for plants and animals and as a source for minerals.

KNOW It All!

The highest mountain in the world is Mount Everest. It rises about 5 1/2 miles (8.9 kilometers) above sea level.

Scientists say the earth's mountains are millions of years old. The youngest mountains have rugged, sharp peaks. Older mountains are smoother, with rounded tops. These older mountains have been worn down by wind and rain over millions of years.

But all mountains begin to wear away, or **erode**, even while they are rising. Rainfall washes away tiny pieces of rock. The wind carries away dust and dirt.

Water seeps into cracks in the rock and freezes. Ice takes up more space than water, so it forces the cracks open. This happens over and over until rocks break off and fall down the mountainside. After millions and millions of years, all of these forces wear away the mountains.

There are five different kinds of mountains.

Fold mountains form when sections of the earth's crust meet head-on. This makes layers of rock in the crust crumple and fold. They often make wavelike patterns.

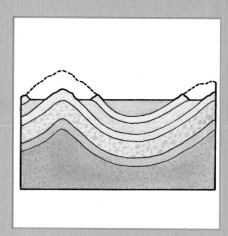

fold mountain

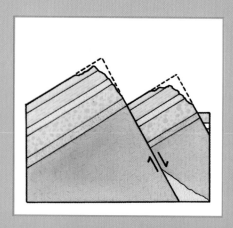

fault-block mountain

Fault-block mountains form when earthquakes make the earth's crust break into large blocks that are tilted or pushed out of place.

Dome mountains form when forces inside the earth push the earth's crust up into a huge bulge or dome.

Erosion mountains form when rivers or glaciers flow over a high, flat area of rock. They wear it away to form peaks and valleys.

Volcanic mountains form when molten rock from deep within the earth erupts. It pushes up through the earth and piles up on the surface.

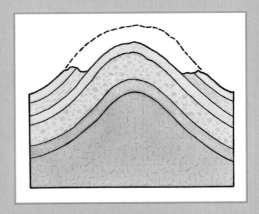

dome mountain

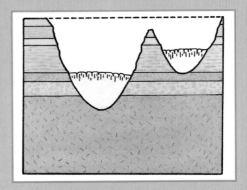

erosion mountain

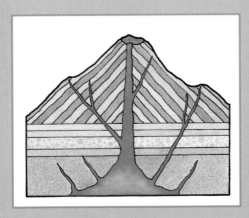

volcanic mountain

Why Do Mountains Explode?

Mount Hekla, in Iceland, shoots fiery hot rock into the air.

Volcanoes begin deep inside the earth.

A volcano is a special kind of mountain that actually builds itself! It is made of red-hot rock that pushed up out of a crack in the earth.

A volcano begins deep inside the earth when the force of hot gas pushes melted rock up. With a loud, deep rumble, the ground begins to shake and burst open. Fiery hot rock can shoot into the air, and melted rock may flow out of the earth. With the volcano, there may be earthquakes and explosions. Huge clouds of smoke and ash may fill the air.

The melted rock is called **magma** (MAG muh). Magma that pours out onto the earth's surface is called **lava** (LAH vuh). Some lava is as thick as syrup, and some is as thin as soup. As thin lava cools, it hardens into smooth sheets of rock.

Glowing hot lava flows out of and across the earth.

Thicker lava cools into rough, jagged sheets.

As more lava pours out of the earth, it falls on the cooled rock. As the ash and rock pile up, a new mountain forms. It forms a cone-shaped mountain with a deep tunnel down its middle.

Cooled lava hardens into smooth sheets of rock.

An Island Is Born

Day after day, huge explosions filled the air. The ocean sizzled as hot rock and ash shot up from the sea floor. Soon, a large mound of dark, melted rock rose out of the water. Far out in the sea, a new volcano was born.

Surtsey is a volcano in the ocean near Iceland that erupted from November 1963 until June 1967. It was so hot, it turned the seawater into pillows of steam.

After it rose above the surface of the ocean, the new volcano was called an island. This island formed in the ocean near the southern coast of Iceland. It is called Surtsey. It is really an underwater volcano, and its bottom lies under the sea.

For four months, huge explosions sent steam and ash into the air. Steam sometimes rose as high as 3.7 miles (6 kilometers). Then flaming hot lava began to flow. When it hit the cold water, the lava cooled and hardened, forming a cone-shaped mountain. The volcano erupted for about three and a half years.

These scientists are measuring plant life on Surtsey.

Today, Surtsey covers an area of nearly 1 square mile (2.6 square kilometers). From a distance, the island appears to have no life on it. But scientists are finding insects and spiders there, as well as plants that started from seeds carried by birds, wind, and water.

The Ground Shakes

The ground shivers, shakes, and rumbles. Whole sections of land move, and even mountains seem to move. What is happening? It's an earthquake!

What causes earthquakes? Earthquakes start in the earth's crust. Pressure builds and pushes rocks until they bend. If you bend a stick long enough, it snaps and breaks. The rocks break, too. When this happens, shivers and quakes rush through the ground. Sometimes a deep rumbling sound fills the air. Sometimes whole pieces of land move.

Thousands of earthquakes that are strong enough to be felt occur somewhere on earth each year. Some people live where small earthquakes happen often. Lamps and hanging plants swing a little. Dishes may rattle. Cars may rock.

In very strong earthquakes, the walls in buildings crack. Bridges collapse, power lines break, and fires begin. In a really bad earthquake, the ground may split open.

People who study earthquakes are called seismologists (syz MAHL uh jihsts). They measure the movement of a quake and the damage it causes. They also try to guess when a quake will happen so they can warn people who might be in danger.

These buildings collapsed during an earthquake in Turkey.

What Are Valleys?

If the highest part of the land is a mountaintop, what do you think the lowest place is? That's right—a valley.

Most valleys begin as land with a stream or river running through it. As the river flows along, it breaks off pieces of the land and carries them away. This deepens the river's path and changes the land beside it.

Over time, water cuts deeper into the earth, making steep walls. Wind and rain wear away at the walls, and this makes the valley widen.

The part of the valley where water flows is called the valley floor. As the valley widens, its floor and walls change shape. Valleys that are long and narrow with steep sides are called canyons or gorges. Valleys in

Many people live in The Rhône Valley in Switzerland.

low-lying plains can be very spread out. Many valleys become so wide that people live in them.

Valleys with very steep walls are called canyons, like Canyon de Chelly in Arizona.

Most valleys are formed by running water, but some form in other ways. Some valleys form where the ground sinks, like the valley the Dead Sea is in between the countries of Jordan and Israel. It is the lowest dry land on the earth. Other valleys can be found high in the mountains where moving piles of snow and ice called glaciers scrape out deep valleys. There are even valleys on the ocean floor.

The valley that the Dead Sea is in is the lowest dry land on the earth.

What Are Plains?

Have you ever traveled across land where the sky seems bigger than the countryside around you? If so, you probably saw a part of the earth called a plain. The land is so flat that you can see for miles and miles.

Most plains are lower than the land around them, but they are not deep like a valley. Many people live on plains because the soil is good for farming. Also, building homes and roads is easier on the flat land of plains than it is in mountainous places.

Plains may be found along a coast or inland. Coastal plains are lowlands that stretch along an ocean's shore. They might be elevated parts of the ocean floor. Or they can be formed by solid materials carried off by water from other coastal plains. Coastal plains usually rise from sea level until they meet higher land, such as mountains.

Inland plains may be found at high levels. The Great Plains, which cover part of the United States and Canada, slope upward from about 2,000 to 5,000 feet (600 to 1,000 meters) above sea level. There they meet the Rocky Mountains.

Thick forests thrive in the damp air along coastal plains. Other plains, like those in which the sky seems so big, have few trees, but they have lots of grasses.

Denver, Colorado, and its surrounding open space are part of the High Plains.

This is how most people imagine a desert, but this is only one type of desert.

What Are Deserts?

The glowing sun glares down on a vast sea of sand. As far as the eye can see, sand stretches in great brown ripples. The air is so hot it seems to shimmer as it rises from the sand. Not even the tiniest green plant is in sight.

Most people picture this endless, hot sandy land when they think of a desert. But there are many kinds of deserts. Some deserts are sandy places with very few plants. Others are flat plains with many kinds of plants. Some deserts are bare spots near a seashore, while others are rocky areas high in the mountains. Some deserts are hot all year around. Others are hot or warm only in summer.

TRY THIS!

1

See how many different colors you can find in this picture of the Painted Desert.

But one thing that is true of all deserts is that they are places where little rain falls. It does rain in deserts, but usually not much. Some parts of deserts get just a sprinkle every few years. Sometimes a desert is so hot that the rain dries up before it reaches the ground! In some deserts, heavy rain can cause sudden floods because the earth can't soak up water fast enough.

One kind of desert is filled with rocks of all sizes.

Scientists say that some deserts were once green and fertile. Changes in climate made the rains stop and turned the land to desert.

Dunes are always changing shape because the wind easily blows around the grains of sand.

The desert is not all dry. An oasis is an area in a desert where underground water comes close enough to the surface to create wells and springs. People live near oases and have farms there.

The dry wind whispers as it passes over high, rocky deserts. Here there is little change. The rocks look the same year after year. But in a sandy desert, you might have a hard time finding the same spot from one year to the next. Hills of sand, called dunes, shift and change shape.

There are two kinds of dunes in the desert. One is usually crescent-shaped. A crescent is like a half circle. This dune builds up gradually into a long slope on the side from which the wind comes. It then drops steeply on the other side.

The second type of dune takes shape along the same direction that the wind blows. It has long, wavy ridges with the same kind of slopes on both sides.

Winds shift the sand from one shape to another. As desert sands shift, the dunes move. As the dunes move, they can cause a lot of damage to any buildings in their path. Desert towns sometimes disappear under shifting sand.

Sometimes the wind moves sand into long, wavy ridges.

The Bottom of the Sea

The sea floor has many mountains, plains, deep valleys, and even volcanoes! Its mountain ranges are longer and wider than those on land. Its valleys are longer and deeper, too.

The earth's surface is covered with a rocky crust. The high parts are the continents and islands, and the low parts are under the sea. The deepest parts are

continent

islands

mountains

trench

long, narrow valleys called trenches. Earth's deepest trench is almost 7 miles (11 kilometers) deep in one spot.

Large mountains rise from the sea floor. In some places, they rise high enough to appear above the water. Many of these mountains are volcanoes. Hawaii is made up of volcanic islands.

Great mountain ranges in the oceans are called ridges. Iceland is part of a ridge in the middle of the Atlantic Ocean. Smaller ridges are found in the Pacific Ocean.

Isn't it surprising that you can find all of these different kinds of land at the bottom of the sea?

The bottom of the sea is not flat. Just like the rest of the earth, it has mountains, valleys, trenches, and volcanoes.

underwater volcanoes

All That Ice

A glacier is a large mass of ice that flows slowly over land in cold polar regions and high mountain valleys. Glaciers begin as snow on a mountaintop. As more snow falls, the weight of the new snow squeezes the snow already there. The snow on the bottom of the pile turns to ice. The ice becomes a glacier.

KNOW It All!

The lowest temperature in the world was measured at Antarctica. It was -128 °F (-89 °C).

Some glaciers look like a river of ice.

There are two kinds of glaciers. One is like a river of ice that slides down from the top of a mountain. The other is like frosting on a cake. It may cover entire mountain ranges and even whole continents.

When a glacier reaches the edge of the frozen land, a large crack will appear in it. With a loud noise like thunder, a huge piece of the glacier falls into the sea and floats away. This piece is called an iceberg.

The land called Antarctica, around the South Pole, is covered by a giant glacier. A sheet of ice that is more than 1 mile (1.6 kilometers) thick covers Antarctica. Under much of this ice is land with mountains, valleys, and plains.

TRY THIS!

How can you tell how much of an iceberg sticks up above the water? Put an ice cube into a glass of water. Look through the side of the glass. You will see that most of the ice cube is

below the surface of the water. The little ice cube in the glass acts just like a giant iceberg in the ocean.

Oceans, Lakes, and Rivers

From space, the earth looks blue because so much of it is covered by water. Are you ready to explore the earth's waters?

There is much to discover. There are huge oceans, long rivers, small streams, and lakes of all sizes.

The World Ocean

Do you think the earth's surface has more land or more water? Would you believe that most of the planet is covered with water? It's true. The land we live on, even the giant continents, are really just like big islands in a huge ocean.

Different parts of the ocean have different names, although all these parts combine to form one giant body of water. The two biggest parts are the Pacific and Atlantic oceans. There are also the Indian and Arctic oceans. Some people call the water near the South Pole the Antarctic Ocean. Can you find these parts of the world's ocean on the globe?

North Pacific Ocean
North America
Arctic Ocean
Asia
North Atlantic Ocean
Europe

South Atlantic Ocean
South America
Africa
South Pacific Ocean
Antarctica
Indian Ocean
Australia

Views of the Northern and Southern hemispheres show the earth's oceans.

Where did the ocean come from? Many scientists say that billions of years ago the outside of the earth was cool, but the inside was fiercely hot. The heat inside the earth caused chemicals to rise to the surface. Some of these chemicals formed water. Over millions of years, the water filled the low parts of the earth.

Sometimes we say "the sea" to mean an ocean or to mean all the world's oceans. But there are also bodies of water that are smaller than oceans that we call seas.

view of much of the earth's oceans from space

What Makes Waves?

On a quiet day, you can hear the waves roll in and splash near the shore. On a stormy day, they thunder.

Waves are made by wind blowing along the top of the water. The water seems to be moving forward—but it really isn't! It only moves up and down. A cork floating on the water would bob up and down as a wave moved under it. This is because the water in a wave does not move forward. Only the shape of the wave moves forward.

When a wave reaches land, it "breaks." The bottom of the wave drags on the

Waves can be a playground in the water.

ground where the water is shallow. The top keeps going. It spills onto the beach, then slides back again. This is the only place where the water in a wave moves forward and back. Everywhere else it just moves up and down.

The biggest waves of all are made by earthquakes under the ocean floor. These waves are called tsunamis (tsoo NAH meez). Far from shore, a tsunami may only reach 1 or 2 feet (30 or 60 centimeters). People on a ship at sea may not even feel it. But as a tsunami approaches land, it can form a wall of water more than 100 feet (30 meters) high.

TRY THIS!

1

Watch a wave move. Tie a piece of rope to a tree or post. Then wiggle the loose end of the rope. You'll see a wave shape travel along the rope. Even though the wave is moving up and down, the rope stays in the same place.

Why Is the Ocean Salty?

You could be out in the middle of the ocean—surrounded by thousands of miles of water—and not have any water to drink when you're thirsty. Why? Because ocean water is full of salt. If you did drink it, it would simply make you more thirsty.

The ocean is salty because rivers dump salt into it. All the rivers that flow down mountainsides and over the land tear loose tons and tons of minerals. Most of these minerals are different kinds of salts. The rivers carry these salts to the ocean.

There's never enough salt in most rivers to make the river water taste salty. But rivers have been dumping salt into the ocean for millions of years. By now, there is enough salt in the ocean to cover all of the land on the earth with a layer of salt hundreds of feet deep!

These cone-shaped mounds are piles of salt. As the seawater **evaporates,** the salt that remains is raked into piles and left to dry in the sun.

Do Your Plants Like Salt?

Can freshwater plants live in salt water?
Here is a way to find out.

You Will Need:

2 small goldfish bowls or large jars, just alike
2 healthy plants, the same kind and size, for
    freshwater aquariums from a pet shop
aquarium gravel
table salt
a tablespoon
a marker, tape, and 2 small pieces of paper

What to Do:

1. Cover the bottom of each bowl with gravel.
Fill each with water and one aquarium plant.

2. Put both bowls in a sunny place, such as a
windowsill, or under fluorescent lights.

3. Put 1 tablespoon of salt into one of the bowls.
Tape a small "Salt" label on that bowl and a "No
salt" one on the other. Watch the plants for a
week. What happens?

The freshwater plant wilts in the salt water. If it is
left long enough, it dies. Plants can live in water of a
certain level of saltiness. They don't grow well if there
is more salt or less salt than they are used to.

The Ocean Meets the Land

Often where the
ocean touches the land,
whether it's the edge
of a tiny island or the
coast of a continent,
there is a beach.

A beach is a stretch
of sand, pebbles, or
rocks. The sea makes
beaches. Waves crash
into a rocky shore for
thousands of years,
tossing the rocks around
and breaking them into
pebbles. Then, for
hundreds or thousands

As the sea tosses rocks around, they rub against
each other and become rounded and smooth.

of years more, the waves grind the pebbles together. In time, the pebbles are ground into tiny grains of sand. Many lakes make beaches this way, too.

This lovely stretch of sand is Lumahai Beach on the Hawaiian island Kauai.

KNOW It All!

The height of a pier seems to change during the day. That's because the water level changes. Tides rise and fall every day as the earth moves. When the water is higher on the pier's supports, it is called high tide. Low tide is when the water level falls.

The Ocean Shapes the Land

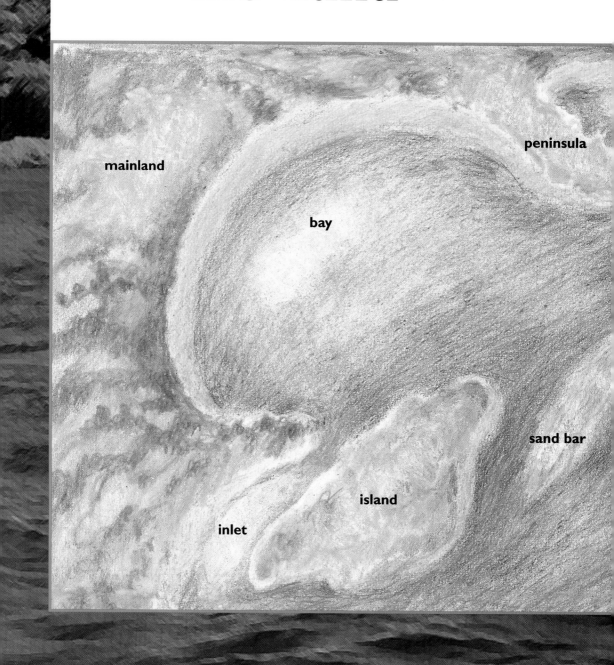

mainland

peninsula

bay

sand bar

island

inlet

When water pokes its way into the land, it creates many different kinds of bodies of water and land areas. Here are some words used to describe such places.

A *bay* is a place where a part of the ocean or a lake pokes into the land. Seen from an airplane, a bay often looks as if a giant has taken a big bite out of the land and water has come in to fill the hole.

An *inlet* is a narrow body of water that pokes into a piece of land or runs between islands. An inlet tends to be finger-shaped.

An area of land that is almost completely surrounded by water is called a *peninsula*. One part of it connects to the mainland.

When waves knock pieces of rock into the water, sometimes they wash up on a beach or settle under the shallow water along a coast. When many pieces of rock collect, a new strip of land called a *sand bar* or *spit* rises from the ocean.

A spring gushes out of the rocks and joins the river below.

spring

tributary

waterfall

Where Rivers Begin and End

High on a mountain, snow melts. Some of the melted snow trickles down the mountainside, finding the easiest path. It is so narrow you could step across it.

Another trickle of water bubbles out from under a rock from underground water called a spring. This trickle joins the melted snow, making a wider, faster-moving stream. It flows down the mountain increasing speed. More streams, or **tributaries**, come together to form a river.

Soil and stones, carried along by the rushing water year after year, cut a groove into the mountainside. The bottom of this groove is the bed of the river. The high sides of the groove are its banks.

The rushing river hurries to the edge of a cliff in the mountainside and falls in a roaring, tumbling, splashing waterfall.

In a steep place near the bottom of the mountain, the fast-moving river has worn away the soft rock. Only bumps of hard rock are left sticking up as the river swirls and foams around them. This part of the river is called the rapids.

The Niagara River rushes over a cliff, forming Horseshoe Falls between the United States and Canada.

KNOW It All!

It has a head at one end and a mouth at the other end. What is it? It's a river! The head is where the river begins. The mouth is where the river ends.

rapids

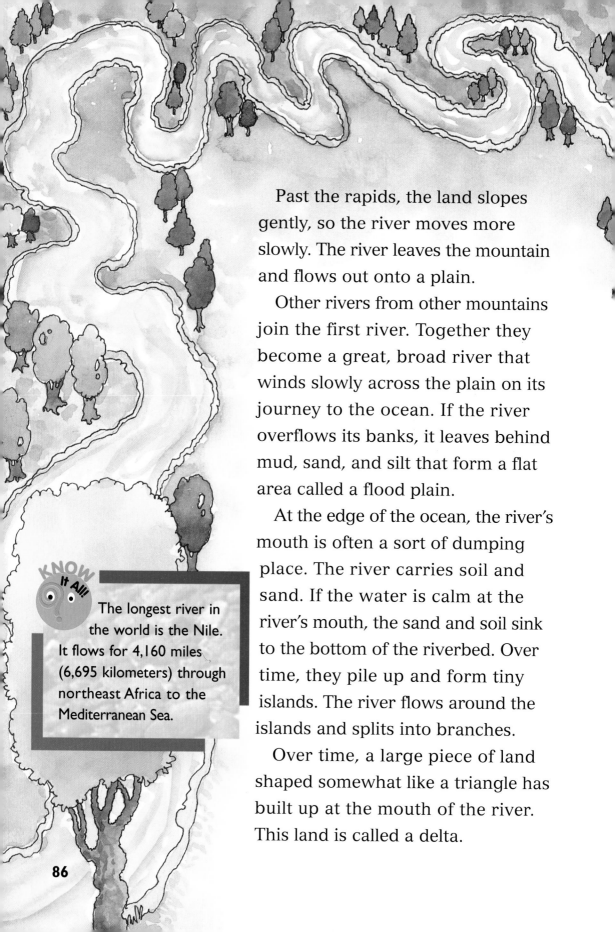

Past the rapids, the land slopes gently, so the river moves more slowly. The river leaves the mountain and flows out onto a plain.

Other rivers from other mountains join the first river. Together they become a great, broad river that winds slowly across the plain on its journey to the ocean. If the river overflows its banks, it leaves behind mud, sand, and silt that form a flat area called a flood plain.

At the edge of the ocean, the river's mouth is often a sort of dumping place. The river carries soil and sand. If the water is calm at the river's mouth, the sand and soil sink to the bottom of the riverbed. Over time, they pile up and form tiny islands. The river flows around the islands and splits into branches.

Over time, a large piece of land shaped somewhat like a triangle has built up at the mouth of the river. This land is called a delta.

KNOW It All!

The longest river in the world is the Nile. It flows for 4,160 miles (6,695 kilometers) through northeast Africa to the Mediterranean Sea.

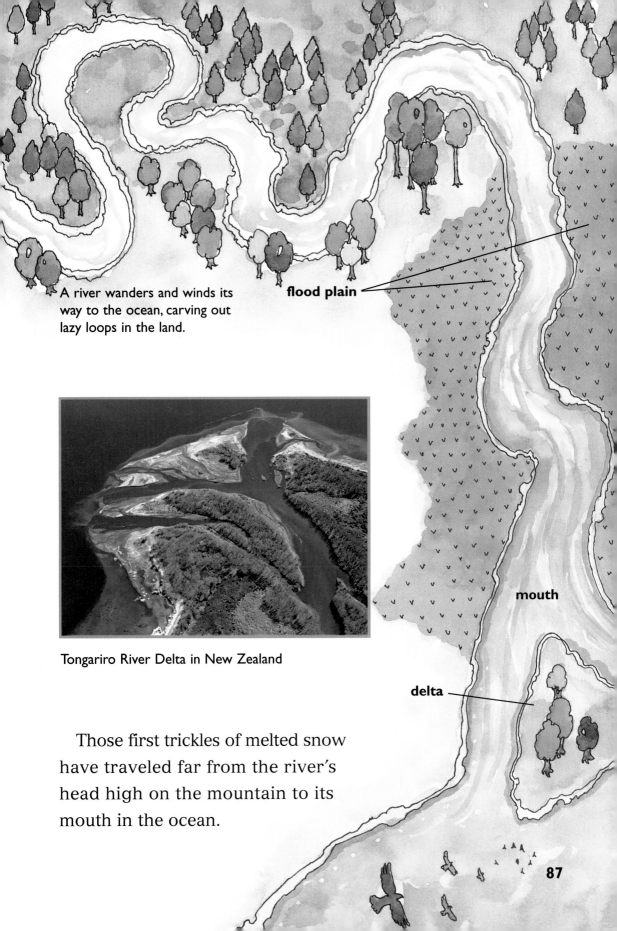

A river wanders and winds its way to the ocean, carving out lazy loops in the land.

flood plain

mouth

delta

Tongariro River Delta in New Zealand

Those first trickles of melted snow have traveled far from the river's head high on the mountain to its mouth in the ocean.

Follow the River

Now that you know the parts of a river, see if you can help this student label her project of a river system.

See answers on page 89.

1. delta   4. waterfall   6. rapids
2. mouth   5. flood plain   7. tributary
3. spring

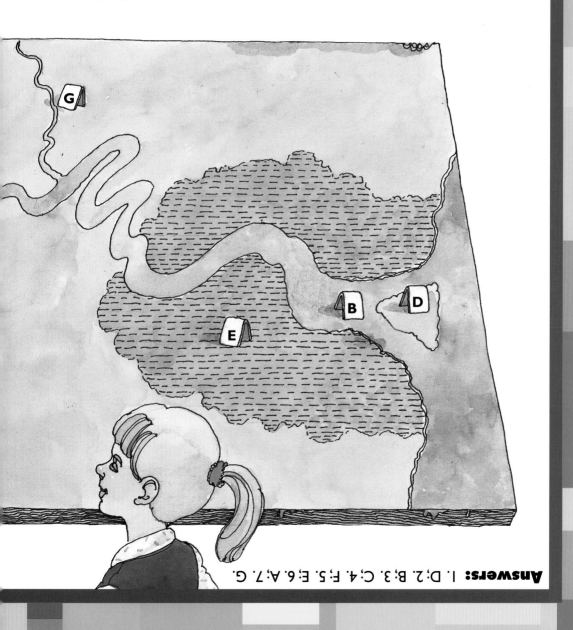

The São Francisco River in Brazil sometimes floods villages on its banks.

Why Do Rivers Flood?

People are shouting, "The water is rising. The river has reached the streets! Get to higher ground. It's a flood!"

A flood happens when water runs over land that is usually dry. Rivers most often flood. Normally, much of the rain that falls on land runs into the nearest river. Water from melting ice and snow also runs into rivers. So, when there is a long, heavy rain, or lots of melting ice and snow, millions of tons of water may pour into a river.

Just as a bathtub will overflow if you keep running water into it, the river soon spills over its banks and floods the land.

Some rivers flood regularly. The people who live near them prepare for floods by piling bags of sand along the riverbanks. This keeps some of the water from spilling over the banks.

Sometimes lakes and seacoasts flood. **Hurricanes** and other bad storms can cause floods along the seacoast. Their strong winds push great waves far onto the land. Soon, much of the shore is underwater.

Unusually heavy rain has caused a river to burst its banks, flooding the land.

a lake in
Germany

What Are Lakes?

A lake is water that has land all around
it. Some lakes are so big that we can't see
the other side. Lake Superior in North
America is the largest freshwater lake in
the world. It spreads over more than 31,700
square miles (82,100 square kilometers).

Some bodies of water called seas are
actually lakes because land surrounds
them. The Caspian Sea, for example, is
the world's largest saltwater lake. This
lake, which lies between Europe and
Asia, stretches for 143,630 square miles
(372,000 square kilometers).

Most lakes are just holes in the ground that are filled with water. Glaciers dug many such holes. Long ago, these huge rivers of ice flowed out of the north and covered many parts of the world. As the gigantic glaciers slid slowly along, they gouged out great pits and made valleys wider and deeper. Then, when the glaciers began to melt, the water filled up many of the holes, forming lakes.

KNOW It All! What's the difference between a lake and a pond? A pond is a very small body of water. It is usually shallow enough for sunlight to reach the bottom.

This lake, Glacial Tarn, is in Cascade National Park in Washington.

Lake Eyre in southern Australia is a dry lake. It fills with water only after heavy rains.

Some lakes form when part of the earth caves in, leaving a hole. This happens mostly in places where the ground is limestone. Year after year, rain dissolves away the soft limestone, forming caves and tunnels.

Finally, the tops of these tunnels cave in, leaving what is called a sinkhole. Rain or water from underground springs and streams fills the sinkhole, and it becomes a lake.

Part of a river can also become a lake. Sometimes a river deposits so much mud

A few lakes, such as
Crater Lake in Oregon,
are extinct volcanoes
that have filled up with
rain water.

and sand that the water backs up and
forms a natural lake. People may make a
lake by building a dam. A dam causes
the flowing water to spread out over the
river's banks and form a lake.

TRY THIS!

1

Ask an adult to fill a glass
jar with water from a lake.
How clear is the
water? Let it stand for an
hour. Then check to see
how much dirt and sand
have settled on the
bottom of the jar.

Why Are Lakes Important?

You probably know that lakes give us food and drinking water. But did you know that lakes offer transportation and energy sources?

Many lakes are important for fishing. People who live near Lake Titicaca (tee tee KAH kah) in South America live simply by raising their own food crops and catching fish from the lake. Other lakes,

oil wells in Lake Maracaibo

like Lake Winnipeg in Canada, support large fishing **industries.**

Lakes are important for shipping, too. North America's Great Lakes are connected with each other and to the Atlantic Ocean. Ships from all over the world can use the lakes to bring things to the many large cities around the lakes.

Lake Maracaibo (mah ruh KY boh), the largest lake in South America, has many

oil wells in its waters and along its shores. Under the bottom of the Caspian Sea, north of Iran, oil and natural gas have been found.

Lake Baikal

Finally, lakes are important to wildlife. For example, Lake Baikal (by KAHL) in Russia is home to many kinds of wildlife found only in that area. These include a fish called the golomyanka and the Baikal seal, one of the few kinds of seals that live in fresh water. Lake Victoria is the largest lake in Africa and the second largest in the world. Flamingos and other birds feed along the edges of the water. Lake Victoria is also known for its many kinds of tropical fish.

These flamingos are feeding in Lake Ndudu in Tanzania.

Water from Underground

Not all of the earth's water is in lakes, ponds, rivers, and oceans. A lot of it is beneath your feet—down in the ground.

Rain falls. Snow melts. Much of the water seeps into the ground. It passes through holes and cracks in the soil until it reaches solid rock. The water can't trickle any farther down, so it spreads out, filling every nook and cranny underground.

The top of this underground water is called the water table. When there is a lot of rain, the water soon fills all the open spaces underground. Then the water table gets higher.

In some places, the water table comes all the way to the top of the ground.

Did you know that there is a lot of water in the ground beneath your feet?

rock

rock

spring

water table

lake

KNOW It All!

Geysers (GY zuhrs) are the earth's hot-water fountains. They are found near places where cold water from a river or lake drains down into the ground until it reaches hot rocks deep in the earth's crust. The hot rocks turn the water into steam. The steam pushes up through cracks in the earth and comes shooting out into the air. Some geysers erupt every few months. Others go off several times an hour. Some of the most famous geysers shoot hot water and steam more than 100 feet (30 meters) into the air.

Then, water bubbles out and makes a natural fountain called a spring. Sometimes a spring is the start of a river.

Underground water is usually cool and clean and good to drink. People often dig wells to get this water. There is some underground water almost everywhere in the world—even in deserts. But in a desert, the water is often very, very far down underground.

water table

Who Studies the Waters?

Many scientists study the ocean, looking into the secrets of the sea. They study how the ocean moves and how it affects the atmosphere. They study the living things in the sea and the shape of the ocean floor.

oceanographers taking water samples for testing

Scientists who study the ocean are called **oceanographers** (OH shuh NAHG ruh fuhrz). Sometimes they work aboard ships. Some wear diving suits and air tanks to explore underwater. Others use small submarines. They use underwater cameras to take pictures of the ocean's floor and the plants and

**marine biologist studying
a great white shark**

animals that live in the ocean. Sometimes they use robots to bring up samples of the mud and sand for study. Some scientists study the direction and strength of waves, tides, and currents.

Oceanographers called **marine biologists** study the plants, fish, and animals that live in the ocean, lakes, and rivers. They keep track of their health and growth patterns.

Oceanographers called **seismologists** (syz MAHL uh jihsts) study earthquakes on the ocean floor. One cause of earthquakes is volcano eruptions, so seismologists often keep track of volcanic activity.

**seismologist studying
volcanic rocks**

Air, Wind, and Clouds

People float on water when they swim.
Clouds float in air and move across the
sky. What are clouds? Why do they float
above us? What pushes them across the sky?

What Surrounds the Earth?

Long ago, people believed the sky was a roof that stretched over the earth. Today, we know that a thick layer of air surrounds the earth like the skin on an

Clouds are part of the atmosphere around the earth. Outside our atmosphere is space.

orange. But unlike an orange skin, the air moves around the earth, and it extends far above the earth's surface. This moving cover of air is a mixture of gases called the earth's **atmosphere** (AT muh sfihr).

Air covers the earth everywhere. The pull of **gravity** holds it there. Near the earth, the air is thick, or heavy. Farther away from the earth, the air becomes thinner. Farthest away from the earth's surface, the air thins and disappears altogether. Where this happens is where space begins!

KNOW It All!

Without air, the earth and everything on it would be silent. Sound travels through the air.

The earth's atmosphere is made of several layers. We live in the part called the *troposphere*.

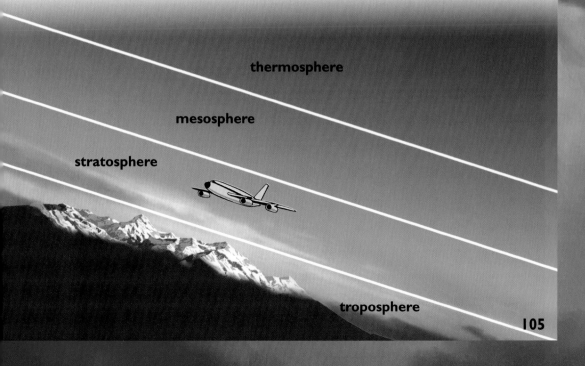

thermosphere

mesosphere

stratosphere

troposphere

Dust in the sky can make a sunset even brighter.

What Color Is the Sky?

If you could stand on the moon and look at the sky, it would always be dark black. This is because the moon has no air. If the earth had no atmosphere, our sky would stay dark, too. Instead, the sky over the earth is dark only at night when the sun doesn't shine.

Sunlight is made up of red, orange, yellow, green, blue, indigo, and violet light. These colors scatter when they hit the earth's air. Some of them scatter more than others. Red, orange, and yellow light scatter the least. Blue scatters so much that it spreads to fill the sky.

That line in the distance where the sky seems to meet the earth is called the horizon. When the sun is near the horizon, sunlight must travel farther through our atmosphere. This makes blue and most other colors scatter too much to be seen. But red, orange, and yellow are scattered just enough to make a beautiful sunrise or sunset. Dust from **pollution**, forest fires, and volcanoes can help make a brighter red or orange sunrise or sunset. The dust makes the other colors scatter even more.

The place where the sky and the earth seem to touch is called the horizon.

What Is Air Made of?

Air doesn't seem to be made of anything. It has no color, taste, or smell, and you can see right through it. But air is made up of things. It is made of many kinds of gases. And these gases are made up of tiny bits called molecules.

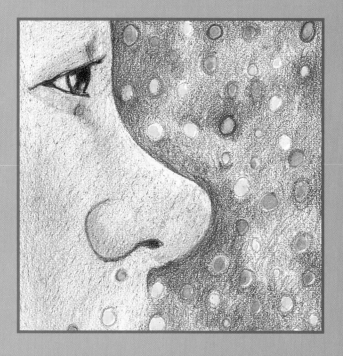

Actually, everything on the earth is made up of molecules. Solid things, such as plants, animals, and rocks, are made of molecules. So are liquids, such as water, and gases, such as the ones in air.

In solids, the molecules are packed close together and hardly move. In liquids, the molecules are farther apart and move faster. In gases, the molecules are very far apart and zip about rapidly. That's why gases are so light that you can't see them.

For us, the most important gas in the air is **oxygen** (AHK suh juhn). We breathe to get oxygen into our bodies. Almost every kind of animal and plant in the world must have oxygen, or it will die.

Only about one-fifth of the air is made up of oxygen. Most of the air—nearly four-fifths—is nitrogen. The rest of the air is made up of many different gases. Water vapor and dust float in the air, but they are not part of the air.

If air is just floating gases, why doesn't it float away into space? Because the earth's gravity pulls at the air just as it pulls at you. The air can no more float off into space than you can!

TRY THIS!

1

You can see that air is made of something. Turn a glass upside down and push it straight down into a bowl of water. The water won't fill up the glass because air is trapped in it.

Turn the glass on its side. You will see the air rush out of the glass. Then the glass will fill with water because air isn't taking up space inside it.

How Does Air Push?

Just as a fish lives in water, you live in an ocean of air. All that air is heavy. Its weight pushes against you in all directions, even though you can't feel it. See for yourself how air pushes.

You Will Need:

a drinking glass (made
   of glass, not plastic or
   paper)
water
a piece of stiff, flat
   cardboard
a sink or a large pan

What To Do:

1. Fill the glass nearly to the top with water.

2. Cover the top of the glass with the piece of cardboard.

3. Hold the cardboard in place and turn the glass upside down. Do this over a sink or a large pan in case the cardboard slips.

4. Move your hand away from the cardboard. What happens?

Did you think the water would push the cardboard away and spill out? Several things are working together to keep that from happening. One of them is that all the air pushing on the bottom of the cardboard weighs more than the water in the glass. That weight pushes against the cardboard, just as that ocean of air pushes against you.

What Makes the Wind Blow?

The wind moves over the land. It sways the tall grass in meadows and rustles leaves on trees. It ruffles your hair. In a storm, it whirls and roars. Wind can change a cloudy day into a sunny one by pushing clouds along. Wind is moving air. And it is the sun that makes air move.

The earth spins around like a big top. As it spins, each part of the earth, in turn, comes into the sunlight. The sun's light warms the earth, and the earth warms the air. The heat makes the molecules of gas in the air move faster and spread

apart. This warm air rises up like a big, invisible cloud. It rises because warm air weighs less than cool air.

As the warm air rises, cool air from other places flows in to replace the warm air. This moving cool air is the wind. When you feel the wind blow, you are feeling the movement of cooler air pushing in to take the place of the warm air that rose up into the sky.

What happens to the warm air? It cools and then sinks back to the ground. There it takes the place of warmer air, and all the same changes happen over again!

KNOW It All!

Air has weight. The weight of the air pressing on the earth is called air pressure (PREHSH uhr). When warm air rises, it puts less pressure on whatever is under it. Such an area is said to have low air pressure. Cooler air weighs more and presses down more on the earth. When it moves in, we say there is high air pressure.

Wind

When the air seems calm, and you can't feel a wind, it doesn't mean that the wind has stopped blowing everywhere. There are always many winds keeping the air around the earth moving. In one place, there may be a soft breeze from the north. In another place, there may be strong gusts from the south.

Two different winds may blow near the same area at once. Near the ground, one wind may be pushing flags in one direction. But higher in the sky, another wind may be making the clouds scurry in another direction.

The fastest winds are high above the clouds, several miles up into the sky. These winds are called jet streams. Often, jet streams are connected. They form one huge, rushing river of wind that circles the earth, sometimes at speeds of more than 200 miles (320 kilometers) an hour. When an airplane takes off for a long trip, the pilot may head up into the jet stream because it can give the plane a powerful push.

How Much Is the Wind Blowing?

TRY THIS! 2

A wind sock can tell you how much the wind is blowing and in which direction. Use these directions to make your own.

You Will Need:

a long sleeve from an
   old shirt
thin, flexible wire
a stapler
string
an adult's help

What To Do:

1. Measure the wire to fit around the shoulder part of the sleeve. Form the wire into a circle to fit the sleeve opening.

2. Tie one end of the string around the wire.

3. Staple the edges of the sleeve over the wire. (Be sure the staples are close together.) Leave the long end of the string hanging out. Now you have a wind sock.

4. Tie the wind sock to a tree or post.

5. Watch the wind sock for several days. Some days the sock will hardly move. Other days, the wind will blow right through it and make it stand out almost straight.

In which direction does the wind tend to blow most often? Move your wind sock. Is one place around your house windier than the others?

How Hard Is the Wind Blowing?

Wind has many different names, depending on how hard it is blowing. On these pages, you will find out how to tell how hard the wind is blowing by watching what it does.

And you will learn some of the names we give to the different speeds of wind.

In calm air, smoke rises straight up. The wind is blowing less than 1 mile (1.6 kilometers) per hour.

In a moderate breeze, small branches sway, and dust and paper blow about. Wind speed is 13 to 18 miles (21 to 29 kilometers) per hour.

In a strong breeze, big branches sway, and umbrellas are difficult to use. Wind speed is 25 to 31 miles (39 to 49 kilometers) per hour.

In a moderate gale, whole trees sway, and it is hard to walk against the wind. The wind speed is from 32 to 38 miles (51 to 61 kilometers) per hour.

A fresh gale breaks twigs off trees and makes walking very difficult. Wind speed is 39 to 46 miles (63 to 74 kilometers) per hour.

A strong gale can blow shingles off roofs and damage buildings. Wind speed is 47 to 54 miles (76 to 87 kilometers) per hour.

A whole gale will uproot trees and often do much damage to buildings. Wind speed is 55 to 63 miles (89 to 101 kilometers) per hour.

What Storm Has an Eye?

A hurricane (HUHR uh kayn) is a huge, whirling circle of wind and rain. But in the center of all this wind and rain, the air is calm. This calm hole is called the eye of the hurricane.

A hurricane begins over the ocean, near the **equator** (ih KWAY tuhr), where the air is very hot, wet, and still. The heated air begins to rise and whirl around. As the great masses of the air rise up, towering rain clouds form.

The winds swirl faster in a giant circle around the center of calm, warm air. The

storm is called a hurricane when its winds are stronger than 74 miles (119 kilometers) per hour.

Some people in the path of a hurricane experience what seems like two storms. First, the front of the circle hits. The blowing wind and rushing rain sound like steady thunder.

After the front of the circle passes over, the eye of the hurricane arrives. The wind dies down. The rain stops. The air grows hot and still. It may take an hour or more for the eye to pass over. Then the back of the circle arrives. Once more, the wind blows and the rain pours. Finally, the hurricane passes, carrying the wind and rain to another place.

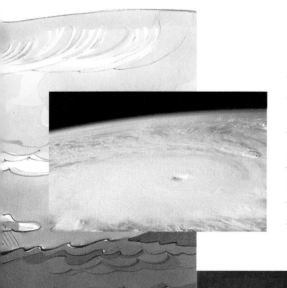

The wind of a hurricane is terrible indeed. It causes huge ocean waves. If these waves reach land, they can cause sudden, terrible floods. If hurricane winds blow over land, they can tear up trees by the roots and push over buildings.

What Are Twisters?

A tornado is a spinning, whirling wind that forms a long tube.

A thick, dark cloud forms in the sky. Warm air from near the earth rises rapidly toward the cloud. At the bottom of the cloud, the air starts spinning. This wind spins and twists and drops down into the shape of a long tube, or funnel. This wind is called a tornado (tawr NAY doh).

The funnel may touch the earth's surface. When a tornado touches ground, it can be dangerous. It can pick up heavy machinery and toss it far. The winds of a tornado rip roofs from houses and uproot large trees.

Tornadoes can happen in many parts of the world. But most tornadoes happen over the central United States. People have recorded whirlwinds about 300 miles (480 kilometers) per hour there.

Here's how to create your own colorful tornado in a bottle. Fill a plastic soda bottle halfway with water. Add tiny pieces of colored paper or confetti. Cover the top of the bottle with a piece of tape and use a pencil to poke a hole in the middle of the tape big enough for the water to flow through. Turn an empty bottle of the same kind upside down on top of the first bottle. Tape their openings together tightly with waterproof tape. Turn the bottles so that the one with water is on top. Gently swirl the water around faster and faster, then stop. The water and tiny pieces of paper whirl like a tornado as they flow into the bottom bottle.

A tornado is a whirling wind that reaches down from the clouds and touches the ground. But dust devils and sand pillars are whirling winds that go from the ground up into the sky. They are much smaller than a tornado.

dust devil

What Are Clouds?

Clouds sometimes look like gobs of whipped cream in the sky. Sometimes they look like soft feathers. But what are clouds?

A cloud is billions and billions of tiny drops of water or ice crystals clustered together. Some clouds are all water, some are all ice, and some are a mixture.

You might think the water and ice would be so heavy it would fall to the

When you sweat on a hot, sunny day, you're helping to make a cloud. When a mud puddle dries up in the sunshine, it's going to become part of a cloud, too.

ground. But the drops are so tiny that the air holds them, and breezes keep them floating in the air.

The water that makes clouds comes from the earth. Every day, the heat of the sun dries up tons and tons of water from everywhere on the earth. All this water is turned into water vapor, which is water in the form of gas. This gas floats up into the air. But as it rises higher and higher, it begins to cool. When it cools enough, it turns back into water or ice. Then, tiny drops form around tiny, tiny bits of dust in the air.

These drops make up the clouds.

TRY THIS!

1

You can make a cloud! All you need is a cold day. Just open your mouth and puff into the cold air. For just a moment, you'll see a cloud. It's a small, white patch in the air, a real cloud. Clouds are made when warm, moist air hits cold air.

Stratus clouds look like thin sheets.

Why Don't All Clouds Look Alike?

There are many different kinds of clouds, and each kind has a name. Most clouds are named for their shape.

The clouds that look like great sheets pulled across the sky are called stratus (STRAY tuhs) clouds. These are the kinds of clouds that are closest to the ground. They form when a layer of warm air rolls over a layer of cooler air. Together they form a thick sheetlike layer.

Cumulus clouds look like fluffy balls of cotton.

The clouds that look like fluffy balls of cotton or scoops of ice cream are called cumulus (KYOO myuh luhs) clouds. Cumulus clouds that rise high into the

Cirrus clouds are thin and wispy.

KNOW It All!

Strato means "sheetlike" or "forming low, horizontal layers." *Cumulo* means "pile" or "heap." *Cirrus* means "curl."

cirrus

cumulus

stratus

air and grow dark and heavy with rain are the kinds of clouds that cause thunderstorms.

The highest clouds of all look like thin, wispy streaks or curls. They are so high up in the air, where the air is cold, that they are made of ice droplets. These clouds are called cirrus (SIHR uhs) clouds.

TRY THIS!

1

How many images can you find in the clouds? Look outside on a cloudy day. Can you find dragons, mountains, or birds? Ask a friend to help you find a few animal shapes.

127

What Is Fog?

Eeee-rump! Eeee-rump! The sound of a foghorn echoes in the night. A thick, gray fog creeps in from the ocean and settles over the waterfront. You can hardly see your hand in front of your face. It seems as if you are in the middle of a cloud.

As a matter of fact, that's just what fog is. It's a cloud of tiny water drops that touches the earth, instead of floating high in the sky.

Fog almost hides the
Golden Gate Bridge
across San Francisco Bay.

Like every other kind of cloud, fog forms when warm, moist air meets cool air. Fog often forms when warm, moist air passes over the cold water of an ocean, lake, or river. The warm air quickly cools. Then the water vapor in it becomes millions of tiny drops—a cloud that rolls in from the water and spreads out over the land.

Fog forms over the land in much the same way when ground that has been warm all day begins to cool off. As the warm air above the ground cools, the water vapor in the air turns into tiny drops of water. A fog hugs the ground.

Can You Make Clouds?

Water is always present in the air around you, even when you can't see it or feel it. This experiment shows how clouds form when cold air and warm air come together.

You Will Need:

a drinking glass (glass or metal—not paper or plastic)

ice cubes

a spoon

What To Do:

1. Do this experiment near a sink or a tub. While you work, run the hot water. This will make sure there is lots of water vapor in the air around you.

2. Fill the glass halfway with cool water and dry the outside of the glass. Drop the ice cubes into the water and stir slowly. After a few minutes, feel the outside of the glass. Is it wet and cold?

3. What happened? The outside of the glass was dry before. Now the warmth from the running hot water has made the air wet nearby. The air is filled with water vapor. When some of this warm water vapor touched the cold glass, drops of water formed.

Clouds form in the same way. When warm air with water vapor in it meets cold air, clouds begin to form.

Weather

Somewhere on the earth right now, it is cloudy and rainy. Somewhere it is sunny. Somewhere it is dark, windy, and snowing.

What is the weather today where you are? Is it raining? Does it look as if it's about to snow? Is the sun shining?

Do you ever talk about the weather? Many people do. Almost everyone cares about the weather.

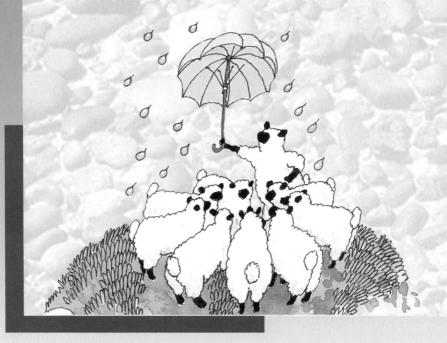

Rain Is Recycled

Rain falls from clouds, but the water in the clouds comes from water on the earth. How does that happen?

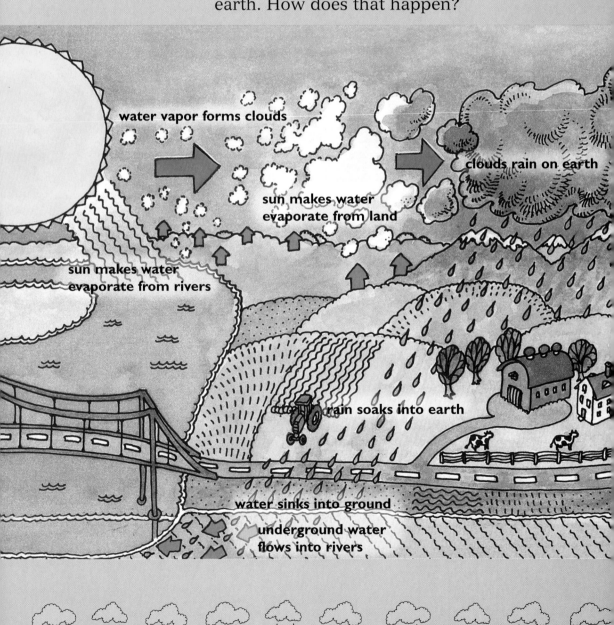

water vapor forms clouds

clouds rain on earth

sun makes water evaporate from land

sun makes water evaporate from rivers

rain soaks into earth

water sinks into ground

underground water flows into rivers

The earth is covered with water—in lakes, streams, ponds, rivers, puddles, and huge oceans. Even the earth's plants and animals have water in them.

Every day, the sun dries up tons of this water, turning it into vapor. The warmth makes the vapor rise. It rises so high that it cools and forms clouds made of water and ice drops. As the drops get larger, they become too heavy to stay in the air. They fall as rain or snow.

Some of the rain and snow soaks into the soil and is used by plants. Some collects in streams or rivers that flow into the ocean. The sun warms it up and turns it into water vapor again. This water cycle happens over and over. The earth is always recycling its water!

KNOW It All!

To recycle something is to make it usable again. Did you know the earth has been recycling water since time began? The water we use today is the same water that the dinosaurs used!

How Much Rain Fell?

Listen to a weather forecaster on a radio or television, and you'll hear how many inches of rain fell during a storm. How does the forecaster know how much rain fell?

Scientists measure rainfall with an instrument called a rain **gauge** (gayj). Rain falls into the gauge. When the rain stops falling, scientists measure the amount of water in the gauge. You can make a simple rain gauge to measure the rainfall around your home.

You Will Need:

a large, clean jar with straight sides
a ruler
a rainy day

What To Do:

1. Place the jar outdoors. Put it in an open place away from trees and buildings so that rain can fall directly into it.

2. Bury the jar partly in the ground or pile heavy rocks around it so that it can't move or tip.

3. Leave the jar outdoors until it rains. When the rain stops falling, carefully bring the jar indoors.

4. Hold the jar up and place the ruler along the side, with the lowest numbers at the bottom. Make sure the first mark on the ruler lines up with the bottom of the jar.

5. Read the ruler where the water line is. This will tell you how much rain has fallen. Record the amount in a journal or weather log.

6. Pour out the water, then dry the jar. Put the jar outside again for the next rainfall. Do you think it will rain more, less, or about the same amount as the first time you measured?

Each time the rain falls, people who study the weather record the amount. This is how they learn something about each year's weather patterns and predict next year's rainfall.

What Makes a Rainbow?

Long ago, people thought rainbows were magic. Some people believed a rainbow was a bridge that appeared in the sky when the gods wanted to leave heaven and visit the earth. Other people believed that if you could find the end of the rainbow—where it touched the earth—you would find a pot of gold.

Today we know that a rainbow is made by sunlight shining through drops of water. Sunlight looks white, but it is really made up of many colors. When sunlight enters a raindrop, it breaks up into lots and lots of colors, including violet, indigo, blue, green, yellow, orange, and red. We see these colors in the rainbow. But because the colors blend, we usually see only four or five of them.

For you to see a rainbow during a rain shower, the sun must be behind you, and the rain must be somewhere in front of you. Rays of sunlight break up into colors as they reflect off many drops of falling rain. Together they make a shimmering, curved, colorful rainbow. If the rain is heavy, one or both ends of the rainbow may appear to touch the earth, many miles apart.

Some rainbows form when it isn't raining. Sometimes small rainbows appear in waterfalls, in sprays of water from the sea, or in fountains where the water shoots high.

TRY THIS!

1 On a sunny day, turn your back to the sun. Spray a fine mist of water from a garden hose. You should see a rainbow in the shining spray. What colors do you see in your rainbow?

A rainbow appears in the sky when sunlight shines through drops of water.

Lightning
and Thunder

Thunder and lightning belong together.

BOOM

A flash of light zigs and zags across the sky. Another flash zaps its way to the ground. A loud crack, boom, or rumble sounds soon after. The flash is lightning. The sound is thunder.

The flash we see when lightning snakes through the sky is really a huge electric spark. During a thunderstorm, each tiny drop of water in a cloud becomes electrically charged making the whole cloud charged. When this electrical charge becomes strong enough, it forms a huge electrical spark—lightning.

Lightning can travel in many ways. Sometimes a charge flashes from one

Lightning is a giant electrical spark that flows through the air.

TRY THIS!

1

You can tell how far away a storm is. When you see lightning, count the seconds before you hear the sound of thunder. Every five seconds equals about 1 mile (1.6 kilometers).

KNOW It All!

Lightning strikes high places, trees, water, or metal objects. To keep safe from lightning, stay inside a house, or a large building. If you are outdoors, go to a low spot away from trees. Keep away from water and metal objects.

place to another within a cloud. Other times, electricity rushes between two clouds with electrical charges. Also, lightning can strike the ground.

A flash of lightning heats up the air around it. The heated air spreads or rushes out in all directions. As it swells, it slams into cooler air, making it shake. This is what causes the sound of thunder.

What Makes It Snow?

Take a close look at some snowflakes. You can see that they aren't drops, like rain; or lumps, like hail; or tiny beads, like sleet. They look more like little feathers.

Snow forms when water vapor in clouds freezes. It forms at the top of storm clouds where the air is colder. The frozen water drops grow as more water vapor freezes onto them. They turn into tiny, clear pieces of ice

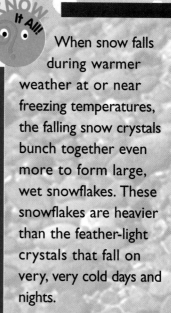

KNOW It All!

When snow falls during warmer weather at or near freezing temperatures, the falling snow crystals bunch together even more to form large, wet snowflakes. These snowflakes are heavier than the feather-light crystals that fall on very, very cold days and nights.

142

called snow crystals. A snowflake is actually a bunch of snow crystals.

When you look at a snowflake through a magnifying glass, you see a beautiful, lacy shape. Even when they may seem the same, no two snow crystals are exactly alike. Some are flat. Others are shaped like long needles. Most look like pieces of lace. Yet, in one way they are almost all the same. Almost all snow crystals have six sides.

Snow can form high in the sky even in summer. But when snow falls in summer, it melts and becomes rain as soon as it reaches warm air lower down.

This is how snowflakes look through a magnifying glass.

Snow crystals blanket the land.

These hailstones have fallen onto a bean crop, destroying and damaging lots of plants.

What Is Hail?

Dark clouds gather and a thunderstorm begins. The patter of rain grows louder and louder. Suddenly, something is pounding on the roof. That "something" is hail.

Hail is lumps of ice and snow. Usually the hailstones look like little beads, but they may be as big as golf balls—or even larger!

Hailstones begin as frozen raindrops in a rain cloud. Wind carries them to a part of the cloud that has some extra cold water drops. Some of the drops land on the already frozen drops, causing them to freeze also.

The frozen drops grow larger as more water drops freeze onto them. This continues as long as an upward wind can support them. The wind keeps them in contact with the extra cold water in the cloud.

Sometimes the wind will slow, and the hailstones will start to fall. But a gust will lift them back up to the extra cold part of the cloud, where they grow even more. Finally, they are so heavy, the wind cannot lift them. The hailstones fall and pound on roofs, grass, and cement.

Weather Watchers

This Australian meteorologist is checking gauges in a weather station.

Everyone is a weather watcher, but almost no one knows how hot, how cold, or how wet it will be tomorrow or next week. But meteorologists can predict the weather.

A **meteorologist** (MEE tee uh RAHL uh jihst) is a scientist who studies the earth's **atmosphere** and its weather. Meteorologists are weather watchers or weather forecasters.

How do meteorologists predict the weather? They search for clues. They check the wind's speed and direction. They record the temperature of the air, the air pressure, and the amount of water in the air.

Meteorologists also gather information from weather **satellites** (SAT uh lytz) in outer space. These satellites circle the earth and photograph clouds and any gathering storms. The pictures are then sent back to the earth.

KNOW It All!
Meteor comes from a Greek word meaning "things in the air."

146

Information also comes from weather stations on the earth's surface. A type of radar called Doppler is used to study winds and storms. It can find approaching storms more than 200 miles (320 kilometers) away.

Meteorologists gather weather reports from all over the world. They use this information to draw weather maps. They also use computers to make **forecasts** (FAWR kastz). You hear their forecasts on television or over the radio. But since the weather changes quickly sometimes, meteorologists often update their forecasts.

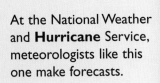

At the National Weather and **Hurricane** Service, meteorologists like this one make forecasts.

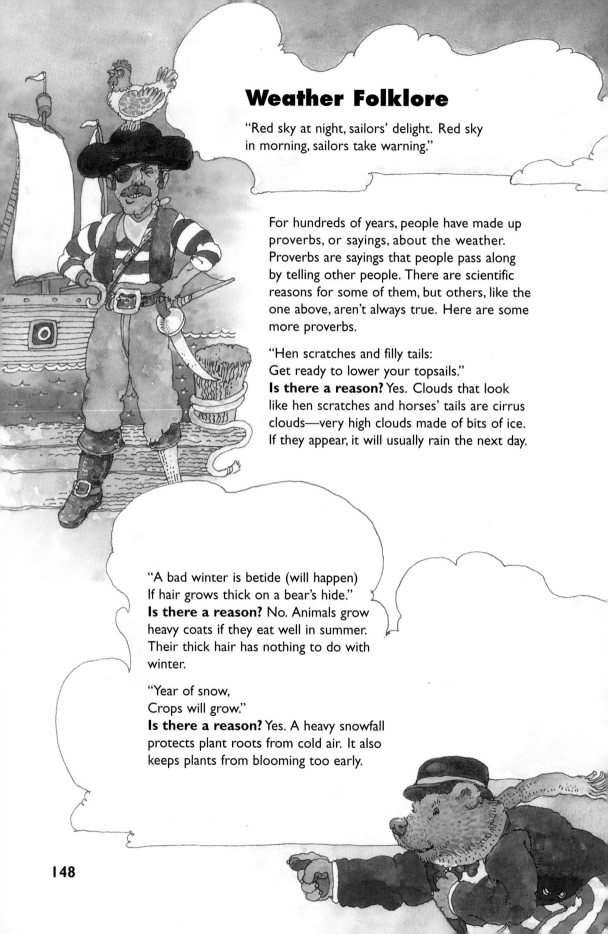

Weather Folklore

"Red sky at night, sailors' delight. Red sky in morning, sailors take warning."

For hundreds of years, people have made up proverbs, or sayings, about the weather. Proverbs are sayings that people pass along by telling other people. There are scientific reasons for some of them, but others, like the one above, aren't always true. Here are some more proverbs.

"Hen scratches and filly tails:
Get ready to lower your topsails."
Is there a reason? Yes. Clouds that look like hen scratches and horses' tails are cirrus clouds—very high clouds made of bits of ice. If they appear, it will usually rain the next day.

"A bad winter is betide (will happen)
If hair grows thick on a bear's hide."
Is there a reason? No. Animals grow heavy coats if they eat well in summer. Their thick hair has nothing to do with winter.

"Year of snow,
Crops will grow."
Is there a reason? Yes. A heavy snowfall protects plant roots from cold air. It also keeps plants from blooming too early.

"When sheep collect and huddle,
tomorrow we'll have a puddle."
Is there a reason? Yes. Animals sense the changing
weather. An approaching storm makes them nervous,
and they huddle together for comfort.

"Seaweed dry, sunny sky;
Seaweed wet, rain you'll get."
Is there a reason? Yes. A piece of dried
seaweed hanging outdoors **absorbs** water
vapor from the air. If it turns wet, the air
is damp, and a storm may be coming.

"If bees to distance wing their flight,
Days are warm and skies are bright.
But when their flight ends near their home,
Stormy weather's sure to come."
Is there a reason? Yes. When the air grows
damp before a storm, bees head back to
the hive for shelter. In fact, in rainy summers,
bees make less honey.

"If the crescent moon lies on her back,
She sucks the wet into her lap."
Is there a reason? No. The moon is
far above the earth's atmosphere. It
can't catch the water in the air!

Make Your Own Weather Center

TRY THIS! 2

Would you like to forecast the weather? On pages 116-117 and 136-137 are directions to make a rain gauge and wind sock. Here is another weather instrument you can make. A barometer measures air pressure. Low air pressure means a change in the weather. High air pressure means good weather.

You Will Need:
a balloon
2 same-size jars
rubber bands
a drinking straw
glue
a flat toothpick
a pencil
scissors
a craft stick

What To Do:
1. Cut off the open end of a balloon. Stretch the rest of the balloon over the top of one jar. Fasten with a rubber band.

2. Flatten the straw and cut one end into a point. Glue the other end to the center of the balloon.

3. Glue a toothpick to the balloon at the edge of the jar. The straw should lie on the toothpick. The straw is the barometer's "needle."

4. Attach a craft stick to the outside of the other jar with a couple of rubber bands so that it reaches about 1 inch (2.5 cm) above the top. If your craft stick doesn't have markings like a ruler, add them along one side, top to bottom.

5. Place the jars so that the cut end of the straw points to the craft stick.

6. Check your barometer at the same time every day. Does it point to a higher or lower mark than the day before? Higher marks mean lower air pressure. Lower marks mean higher air pressure.

You can use your weather instruments to keep track of the weather over time. Ask an adult for a calendar you can write on. Create symbols for the weather. For example, a wiggly line can be clouds, a smiling face can be sunshine. Each day, draw symbols for the day's weather on the calendar.

What Is Climate?

Some places are warm almost every day of the year. Other places are mostly cool and rainy. Other places have changing seasons—spring, summer, autumn, and winter.

Climate (KLY miht) is what the weather is like in the same area over a long period of time. Climate and weather are not the same thing. Weather is what happens in the atmosphere over a short period of time.

The sun, the ocean, and the land all help to make a climate. At the North and South poles, the climate is cold because the sun's rays shine at an angle. Angled rays are not as strong as direct rays.

KNOW It All!

Clues to the earth's climate have been found in giant sequoia trees. When a tree is cut, many growth rings can be seen in the trunk. These rings show whether or not much rain has fallen in a certain year. Thick rings indicate good rain and growth seasons.

Near the **equator,** the sun's rays shine almost straight down. So the climate of most countries near the equator is very warm or hot.

Warm parts of the ocean near the equator often have the wettest climate. This is because in these places the air absorbs the greatest amount of moisture, and it falls as rain.

Sometimes the climate of mountains is cooler than the land around them. In these higher places, warm air rises and cools rapidly. Some parts of mountains are also wetter because warm air is moist. As the warm air rises, it quickly cools. The cool air can't hold a lot of water, so it falls as rain.

A Look at Different Climates

dry, hot climate in a desert in Namibia

There are many kinds of climates in the world. The pictures on these pages give you a glimpse of some different climates. Which one is most like the climate you live in?

cool, dry climate of autumn in New England

icy cold climate
in Antarctica

moist climate in a rain
forest in Australia

Do Climates Change?

Climate is important to people, plants, and animals. It makes a difference in where and how people live and work. It affects the amount of food that can be grown to eat. But did you know that there are things that can change the climate? Natural events and people can cause long-term changes in the climate.

One natural event that can change the climate is a volcano. When a volcano erupts, it throws huge amounts of dust into the atmosphere. The dust may stay in

Some scientists believe that volcanic
eruptions changed the climate long ago.

the air for many years, scattering the sun's
rays and blocking sunlight from the
ground. So a volcanic eruption may actually
cool parts of the earth.

The actions of people have also changed
the climate. The climates of areas that are
now cities have become warmer than
nearby land. This is because large
buildings, streets, and sidewalks hold
heat. Also, **pollution** slows water vapor
from rising into the atmosphere, so most
cities have a slightly wetter climate, too.

Why Protect the Earth?

The earth is full of natural resources—water, air, and land. The earth is also full of life—plants, animals, and people.

We all depend on the water, air, land, plants, and animals to live. So, it is important for people to protect the earth and everything on it.

BEACH CLOSED! Water is polluted.

Using the Earth

People everywhere—including you—are using the earth and its **resources** (ree SAWRS ehz) daily. Look around and see.

We all need water to survive. People use the earth's water to drink and to wash. They use it to grow crops. They fish its oceans, lakes, and rivers.

People use the land. They farm the land to grow food. They clear land to build homes and roads. They mine the land for such minerals as coal, iron, and gold.

People enjoy the earth. They grow gardens and make parks. They go swimming and boating.

How many ways do you use the earth?

The Earth's Natural Resources

What if there weren't an ocean or any lakes, ponds, or rivers? What if there were no plants to eat? What if there were no iron to build things with?

Natural resources include all the things that support life. Sunlight, water, soil, and minerals are all natural resources. There are plenty of some resources, and not so many of others.

Sunlight, for example, cannot be used up. Neither can water. The earth has lots of these natural resources. But some places on the earth have more water, more sunlight, or cleaner water than other places.

Some natural resources can be used more than once. These are called recyclable resources. For example, aluminum can be used to make containers, and the containers can be recycled—used to make something else.

Other natural resources can be used and replaced. Animals can reproduce, so they are replaced with new animals. As trees are used, new trees can be planted.

But some natural resources are replaced so slowly we could run out. For example, people are quickly using up the earth's supplies of coal, oil, and iron. It would take millions of years for the earth to make more of these resources.

People will lose out on things they enjoy, like beaches, if pollution isn't stopped.

What Is Pollution?

Pollution (puh LOO shuhn) is anything that people do that damages the natural environment. For example, if poisonous

garbage discarded along highway

chemicals are not properly thrown away, they can get into the ground, water, or air.

There are many ways that people pollute the earth. When poisonous chemicals, such as paints and fertilizers, are dumped into rivers and lakes, the plants and animals that use that water may become sick or die.

downtown Los Angeles covered in smog

When waste from people and animals gets into the soil and water, the plants and animals that use that soil and water may become sick.

Some pollution damages the air. Smog is one kind of air pollution. It is created by the action of sunlight on exhaust from cars and factories. Very heavy smog can hurt people. Even countries that work to improve their own air can be polluted by air from a neighboring country.

Using the Land Wisely

Every year, there are more people on the earth using more of the earth's resources. If people aren't careful, the resources will be wasted, damaged, or used up.

To make space for the **development** of houses, roads, sidewalks, and parking lots, people cut down trees and other plants. But careful builders leave areas in their developments where they plant trees to replace the ones they've cut. This allows animals to keep their homes or find new ones.

Also, governments protect some prairies, wetlands, forests, and other land from development.

Factories and other buildings can send waste chemicals into the air and water. Laws require builders to be careful so that new buildings don't pollute the air and water.

Developers for Atlanta, Georgia, created this park. Not only does it make the city more beautiful, it is also good for the environment.

Workers remove valuable resources from the land. If too much is taken, the supply will be used up. However, businesses are required to save minerals by using better ways of mining and recycling mineral products. They also substitute more plentiful minerals for scarce ones.

Is the Earth Heating Up?

Some people say the earth is very slowly getting warmer. They say the earth's **atmosphere** (AT muhs fihr) is warming the earth, just as a greenhouse warms plants.

Have you ever seen a greenhouse? It has glass or plastic walls that let the light and

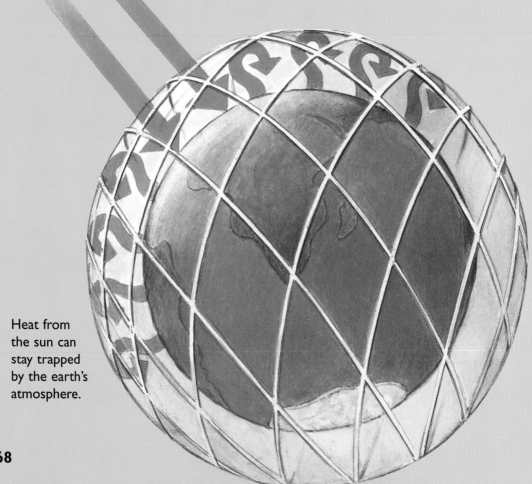

Heat from the sun can stay trapped by the earth's atmosphere.

168

heat of the sun in so plants can grow. Because the walls also help hold in the heat, a greenhouse becomes very warm.

The earth and its atmosphere act like a greenhouse. The earth's atmosphere allows most of the sun's light to pass through it and heat the earth's surface. The earth sends the heat back into the atmosphere. But the atmosphere contains gases, such as **carbon dioxide** (kahr buhn dy AHK syd), that act like greenhouse walls, holding in some of the heat.

When people burn fuel in cars and factories, they send carbon dioxide into the air. Too much carbon dioxide in the atmosphere may prevent more and more of the sun's heat from leaving the ground. This makes the ground and the air around it pretty warm! This is called the greenhouse effect. Some scientists think it is causing problems for our earth.

KNOW It All!

Warmer temperatures would melt some of the ice at the North and South poles. This water would flow into the oceans and cause the water level to rise. This would flood land along coasts all around the world and would completely cover some islands!

How Can People Protect the Earth?

For thousands of years, people have used the earth's land, water, and air. Also, people have also polluted the earth with their waste, harmful chemicals, and other poisons.

Now people all over the world are working to protect the earth. They are working to preserve land, stop **pollution**, save natural **resources**, and protect endangered wildlife. There are many ways to help the earth. You can help, too.

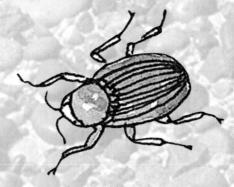

The Three R's

How many things did you use today that were made from trees or plastic? How many of those things did you throw away? How many things did you use that required electricity?

Many things that people use are made from trees or plastic. For example, lots of paper and wooden products are made from trees. Many plastics are made from petroleum, coal, and natural gas. And the more we throw away plastic and paper, the more garbage dumps are needed.

Many things that people use are powered by the earth's natural resources, too. As we use electricity to run refrigerators and other products, minerals are needed to create that electricity.

Many people are worried that the earth's resources are being used up and polluted. With these three R's—reduce, reuse, and recycle—you can help preserve the earth's resources.

Riding a bike saves on gas and the
amount of pollution from car exhaust.

Reduce

- Use fewer paper and plastic products.
  Use cloth towels instead of paper towels.
- Turn off the lights, radio, and TV when
  you're not using them.
- Instead of running water until it's cold,
  use ice cubes. Or keep a pitcher of cold
  water in the refrigerator.
- To save hot water, take showers instead
  of baths.
- If you have a dishwasher, don't use it
  until you have a full load.
- Ride a bike, join a carpool, or take the
  bus or train to save on gas and oil.

You can make fun toys out of used containers, but you should always have an adult's help.

Reuse

- Wash out plastic milk bottles, plastic bags, and aluminum foil, and reuse them.
- Repair and reuse toys and other products.
- Save used paper and plastic to make gifts.
- Use both sides of writing paper.
- Sell or donate goods so someone else can reuse them.

Recycle

- Recycle aluminum cans, glass and plastic containers, newspapers, rubber items, and paper. Recycled materials are used to make new products.
- Use recycled paper to write, paint, and draw.

When you recycle things, you are helping protect the earth.

TRY THIS!

1 What other reasonable R's can you think of? For example, refuse and recover. Refuse to litter. Refuse to buy items that are heavily packaged. Recover resources by buying things made from recycled products.

What Are People Doing to Help?

These people are able to visit and enjoy the Children's Eternal Forest because of the efforts of children in Sweden to protect it.

There are many ways that people help the earth. Some of them restore or preserve resources. Others reduce pollution and reuse resources.

Children in Sweden helped save a rain forest that is halfway around the world from their homes. They wrote letters and talked to people to get them involved, and raised money to help save a rain forest in Costa Rica, Central America.

They even got children from other countries interested in helping, too. Today, the rain forest is called El Bosque Eterno de los Niños, or The Children's Eternal Forest, and serves as a natural wildlife **habitat** (HAB uh tat) for lots of plants and animals.

Another place many plants and animals live is in the ocean, but it isn't always a safe, clean home. A major source of ocean pollution is oil. When oil is accidentally spilled into the ocean, governments, businesses, and people join together to help to clean it up.

After an oil spill, the oil is held inside a floating boom to keep it from spreading while workers, like the one pictured here, scoop it out of the water.

Governments are passing laws to force **industries** to control their pollution or pay large fines. For example, factories can only dump a certain amount of their wastes into the air or into lakes and rivers.

Many people plant trees. The new trees help replace old ones that were cut down to make paper, furniture, or other products. Planting trees also helps preserve soil. Without trees and other plants, fertile soil is easily blown and washed away.

In Kalundborg, Denmark, one company uses another company's waste for energy. A coal-powered plant produces steam and heat to make electricity. In the past, the used steam was released into the air. But now it is channeled to other industries. These industries use the steam for heat as well as other processes.

Every day, while generating electric energy, power plants produce a mineral called gypsum as a waste product. Instead of throwing it away, some plants send the gypsum to another company that uses it to make plasterboard.

In many places, especially in some countries in Europe, people often carpool, or drive together. This helps to reduce pollution.

People who work to be sure that the earth can provide for humans are called conservationists. Conservation (KAHN suhr VAY shuhn) is the protection and wise use of natural resources. Everyone can be a conservationist every day.

This conservationist is working to restore part of the Boise National Forest after a fire.

Keeping Track

Believe it or not, frogs and insects help people learn about how healthy the earth is. Scientists called **naturalists** (NAHCH uhr uh lists) keep track of how many animals there are in the world. In some places, where once they saw thousands of some kinds of

Students stir a stream to gather insects and other specimens to study.

After collecting specimens, the students sort them.

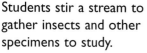

Write to an organization to learn more about endangered wildlife and how you can help. Many organizations collect information about endangered wildlife. One is the International Union for Conservation of Nature and Natural Resources, based in Switzerland. Other groups include the Sierra Club and the National Audubon Society.

animals, now there are hundreds—or only dozens. A change in the number of animals tells scientists that there may also be a change in the environment, the earth, and its resources.

For example, students volunteer to help collect insects from rivers and streams. Then scientists study the insects and record their findings. Too many or too few of one kind of insect could show a change in the environment, possibly an increase or decrease in pollution.

When winter forests in the north turn cold, monarch butterflies fly to warm forests in Mexico. At one time, the people in Mexico noticed fewer monarch butterflies in their forests. Where were they? They weren't visiting because people had cut down the trees and sold them to businesses. The monarchs had lost their winter homes. However, the people in Mexico saved their forests, and the monarchs, by planting new trees.

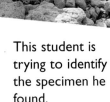
This student is trying to identify the specimen he found.

Get your family and neighbors together to clean up your neighborhood park.

What Can You and Your Friends Do?

1. Adopt part of a beach or neighborhood and pick up litter. If something is recyclable, recycle it.

2. You and your friends can put together a short play or skit. Act out ways to help the earth. Present your play at school or a community event.

3. Make a banner to help others learn about pollution. See if your school or public library will display it.

You and your friends can make a difference.

4. Check to see if any local organizations work to help the earth. Ask if you can volunteer.

5. Start a Recycling Club at your school. Decorate large cardboard cartons to put cans, bottles, and paper in. Ask teachers or the principal if you can place one in classrooms, the lunchroom, and teacher's lounge. Also ask them to help plan how you will empty the boxes. Make a schedule to empty the boxes.

6. Have a contest to see who can build the most interesting piece of art from recycled materials. Use recycled toys, puzzles, and books as prizes.

Someday you will be a grown-up. What would you like to do then to help the earth? Where would you like to live? What kind of house would you build? This big blue ball called the earth is yours to enjoy.

Glossary

Here are some of the words you read in this book. Many of them may be new to you. Some are hard to pronounce. But since you will see them again, they are good words to know. Next to each word, you will see how to say it correctly: **tributaries** (TRIHB yuh TEHR eez). The part shown in small capital letters is said a little more loudly than the rest of the word. The part in large capital letters is said the loudest. Under each word are one or two sentences that tell what the word means.

A

absorb (ab SAWRB)
Absorb means to take in or to soak up.

altitude (AL tuh tood)
The altitude of a place or an object is its height above sea level.

atmosphere (AT muhs fihr)
Atmosphere is the air that surrounds earth.

C

carbon dioxide
(kahr buhn dy AHK syd)
Carbon dioxide is a gas in Earth's atmosphere. People and animals breathe it out and plants absorb it.

climate (KLY miht)
Climate is the kind of weather that a place has over a long period of time.

D

development (dih VEHL uhp muhnt)
Development means something that grows. A housing development is an area where many houses are built and sold at one time.

E

equator (ih KWAY tuhr)
The equator is an imaginary line around the middle of earth halfway between the North and South poles.

erode (ih ROHD)
To erode is to wear away.

evaporate (ih VAP uh rayt)
To evaporate is to change from a liquid to a gas.

F

forecast (FAWR kast)
To forecast is to tell what is going to happen before it happens. A weather forecast lets people know what kind of weather is coming.

fossil (FAHS uhl)
A fossil is the remains or traces of an animal or plant that lived long ago. A fossil may be a print or a bone that has changed to stone.

G

gauge (gayj)
A gauge is an instrument used to measure something. A rain gauge measures the amount of rainfall.

gravity (GRAV uh tee)
Gravity is a force that pulls things toward earth.

H

habitat (HAB uh tat)
A habitat is a place in which a plant or animal lives and grows.

hurricane (HUHR uh kayn)
A hurricane is a huge storm with rain and strong winds. A hurricane has a calm area in its middle called the eye of the storm.

I

industry (IHN duh stree)
Industry is the part of a country's wealth that is invested to produce goods and services.

L

lava (LAH vuh)
Lava is the hot, liquid rock that pours out of an erupting volcano.

M

magma (MAG muh)
Magma is hot melted rock below the earth's crust.

meteorologist (mee tee uh RAHL uh jihst)
A meteorologist is a person who studies climate and forecasts weather.

N

naturalists (NACH uhr uh lists)
Naturalists are people who study animals and plants.

O

oxygen (AHK suh juhn)
Oxygen is a colorless, odorless gas that is in the atmosphere. People and animals need it to live.

P

pollution (puh LOO shuhn)
Pollution is the damage done to air, soil, and water by harmful substances.

R

resource (rih SAWRS)
Resource is a supply of something that is needed, such as oil or timber.

S

sediment (SEHD uh muhnt)
Sediment is tiny pieces of rock, dust, and soil that settle at the bottom of a liquid.

T

tributaries (TRIHB yuh TEHR eez)
Tributaries are small streams that flow into a larger stream or river.

Index

This index is an alphabetical list of important topics covered in this book. It will help you find information given in both words and pictures. To help you understand what an entry means, there is sometimes a helping word in parentheses, for example, **amethyst** (gem). If there is information in both words and pictures, you will see the words *with pictures* in parentheses after the page number. If there is only a picture, you will see the word *picture* in parentheses after the page number.

Illustration Acknowledgments

The Publishers of *Childcraft* gratefully acknowledge the courtesy of the following illustrators, photographers, agencies, and organizations for illustrations in this volume. When all the illustrations for a sequence of pages are from a single source, the inclusive page numbers are given. Credits should be read from top to bottom, left to right, on their respective pages. All illustrations are the exclusive property of the publishers of *Childcraft* unless names are marked with an asterisk. (*)

Cover	Sand angels—© Cathy Melloan; Volcano—Roberta Polfus; Snowflakes—© F. Sauer, Zefa Picture Library*; Lightning—John Deeks*
Back Cover	© F. Sauer, Zefa Picture Library*
1	Roberta Polfus; © F. Sauer, Zefa Picture Library*; John Deeks*
2-3	Field Museum of Natural History (CHILDCRAFT photo); John Sandford; James Conahan
4-5	© Alan Band Associates*
6-7	Robert Masheris; James Conahan; Estelle Carol
8-9	Robert Alley; NASA*
10-11	Robert Alley; John Sandford
12-13	Herb Herrick; Eileen Mueller Neill
14-17	Gerald Witcomb
18-19	© Cathy Melloan*
20-21	Susan Schmidt
22-23	John Sandford; Field Museum of Natural History, Chicago (CHILDCRAFT photo); John Sandford; John Sandford
24-25	Field Museum of Natural History, Chicago (CHILDCRAFT photo); John Sandford; Field Museum of Natural History, Chicago (CHILDCRAFT photo); John Sandford
26-27	E. R. Degginger; CHILDCRAFT photo; WORLD BOOK photo; Field Museum of Natural History, Chicago (CHILDCRAFT photo); © John Gerard*; Field Museum of Natural History, Chicago (CHILDCRAFT photo)
28-29	Sharon Elzuardia; © Zefa Picture Library*
30-31	Eileen Mueller Neill
32-33	Field Museum of Natural History, Chicago (CHILDCRAFT photo); Robert Weldon, Gemological Institute of America*; Robert Weldon, Gemological Institute of America*; Jeffrey Kurtzeman; Field Museum of Natural History, Chicago (CHILDCRAFT photo); Robert Weldon, Gemological Institute of America*; Robert Weldon, Gemological Institute of America*; Field Museum of Natural History, Chicago (CHILDCRAFT photo); Field Museum of Natural History, Chicago (CHILDCRAFT photo); Robert Weldon, Gemological Institute of America*; John Langley Howard and Paul D. Turnbaugh
34-35	Field Museum of Natural History, Chicago (CHILDCRAFT photo); Field Museum of Natural History, Chicago (CHILDCRAFT photo); © Joyce Photographics from Photo Researchers*; Field Museum of Natural History, Chicago (CHILDCRAFT photo); Field Museum of Natural History, Chicago (CHILDCRAFT photo);
36-37	Bill Miller (photo by Ralph Brunke); © Bill Ratcliffe*; CHILDCRAFT PHOTO
38-39	Len Ebert
40-41	James Conahan; Gerald Witcomb; © Bob Fleumer, Zefa Picture Library*
42-43	© David R. Frazier, Tony Stone Images*; © S. J. Krasemann, Photo Researchers*; © DOE/Science Source from Photo Researchers*
44-45	© Sam Ogden/SPL from Photo Researchers*; © Lowell Georgia/Arctic Resources from Photo Researchers*; © David R. Frazier, Photo Researchers*
46-47	Gerald Witcomb; © Alan Band Associates*
48-49	Peter Visscher; George Suyeoka
50-51	© Uniphoto/Pictor*; © Photo Researchers*
52-53	Steven Brayfield, Artisan-Chicago
54-55	© Alan Band Associates*; Roberta Polfus; © C. Bonongton, Woodfin Camp, Inc.*; © Walter Bonatti, Pictorial Parade*; Len Ebert
56-57	© GeoScience Features Picture Library*; © Bob Krist, Corbis
58-59	© Reuters/Archive Photos*; James Conahan
60-61	© Alan Band Associates*; © Photo Researchers*; © Peter Arnold, Inc.*
62-63	© David Rosenberg, Tony Stone Images*
64-65	© Knight & Hunt from Zefa Picture Library*; © Ester Henderson, Photo Researchers*; © Superstock*
66-67	© Zefa Picture Library*; Estelle Carol; © Zefa Picture Library*;
68-69	Gerald Witcomb
70-71	James Conahan; © M. Thonig, Zefa Photo Library*; James Conahan
72-73	The Wright Bros.; © George Ranalli, Photo Researchers*
74-75	James Teason; NASA*
76-77	© Richard Hutchings, Photo Researchers*; Robert Masheris
78-79	© Georg Gerster, Photo Researchers*; John Sandford
80-81	© Zefa Picture Library*; © Superstock*; Kate Salley Palmer
82-83	Kate Salley Palmer
84-85	John Sandford; © Bob Croxford, © Zefa Picture Library*; © Orion Press from Zefa Picture Library*
86-87	John Sandford; © G. R. Roberts*
88-89	John Sandford
90-91	© Ives, Zefa Picture Library*; © Ives, Zefa Picture Library*; Steven D. Mach
92-93	© Vance Henry, Taurus*; © Michael P. Gadomski, Photo Researchers*; Estelle Carol
94-95	© Bill Bachman, Photo Researchers*; James Conahan; John Sandford
96-97	© Vince Streano, The Stock Market*; © J. Polleross, The Stock Market*; © Thomas Kitchin, Tom Stack & Associates*